God East and West

In memory of RJB and JFXH –
who said it better

God
East and West

MICHAEL BARNES SJ

First published in Great Britain 1991
SPCK
Holy Trinity Church
Marylebone Road
London NW1 4DU

British Library Cataloguing in Publication Data

Barnes, Michael 1947–
God east and west.
1. Religions. Doctrines
I. Title
291.2

ISBN 0–281–04524–0

Typeset by David John Services Ltd, Maidenhead
Printed in Great Britain by
The Longdunn Press Ltd, Bristol

Contents

Preface

This book started life as a lecture course at Heythrop College for students of pastoral theology who needed a manageable but accurate account of Indian religions together with some attempt at Christian theological reflection. Almost the only part of the original course which remains is the title. Over the years the content, style and scope have shifted, from a brief consideration of the concept of God to something more inclusive of the great variety of spiritual traditions, East and West. I am extremely grateful to all those who have aided that process of development – from students and friends, who have discussed these ideas with me, to various revered teachers who first opened up for me the many beauties, and areas of darkness, of human religiosity. If I omit to name anyone specifically, it is not because I am unaware of a multitude of debts. Such a list would be enormous. But it seems more appropriate in a book of this type, which aims to chart a personal journey into the realms of inter-faith spirituality, to keep the ponderous apparatus of notes and references to a minimum. I can only hope that 'personal' does not mean idiosyncratic, and that nothing I have written will be considered unworthy of those to whom so many debts are due.

Michael Barnes SJ
Heythrop College
October 1990

INTRODUCTION
Languages of Faith

We cannot study God. We can study how people have experienced God in different ages and cultures, how their scriptures and holy books have interpreted that experience, and what their most precious traditions have taught. We can study people's religious practices: what they do in church and temple and mosque, the way they worship, meditate and pray. We can study the effect that religion has on ethical and social behaviour, the relationship between belief and people's everyday human concerns. But what we cannot study is God, the Ultimate Reality, for God is not an object to be put under the microscope or reduced to the status of the topic of a learned monograph.

This book, however, is not an exercise in the objective study of religions. But neither is it pure theology – a word which comes close to meaning 'study of God' but which more properly applies to a community's attempt to explain its ancient traditions about its experience of God in the face of questions from within or without. In a straightforward and, I hope, cheerfully uncomplicated way, what I have written tries to do both – and therefore requires something by way of explanation.

I am often asked how a Jesuit priest got involved in inter-faith dialogue. The flippant answer (often too tempting to resist) is 'by mistake'; the more considered involves chronicling a long and complicated journey which began with an interest in mysticism, moved on to the study of the meditative traditions of India, and has since shifted into the more practical encounter between different religious communities. The record of Christian academics in the field of religious studies, including at least one of my revered teachers, is thoroughly distinguished and needs no justification whatever. Nowadays their work, and the experience of inter-faith dialogue, is beginning to have an impact on the study of theology. Someone with a foot in both camps naturally wants to aid that process – one which is challenging, sometimes infuriating, but always profoundly absorbing.

Years ago, librarians would probably have classified this book under the heading 'Comparative Religion'. True, much of its subject-matter is an exercise in comparison, taking themes common to Christianity, Islam, Hinduism and Buddhism and seeking the points of convergence and divergence. I hope, however, that there is more to it than that, for it represents a personal journey of understanding (and at times – it must be admitted – of blank incomprehension). Anyone interested in the extraordinary richness of divine activity in the world has to make such a journey, the more so someone committed to making that mystery known. And involved in that journey is the constant need to revise the basis of comparison, to recognize unconscious bias, to delve further into the cultural and historical roots of religious belief.

The same people who want to know how I got started also ask what a Christian theologian has learned from Hindus, Buddhists and Muslims. I can (and often do) rattle off a whole series of insights and ideas – the sort of thing which is necessary to liven up the dry-as-dust academic lecture. Studying world religions is not, after all, a matter of amassing a personal encyclopedia of customs, beliefs and rituals, but of understanding what religion, that curious human phenomenon which is the source of so much power for good and for ill, is all about. At which point the thin line dividing theology from religious studies begins to fade. The inter-faith dialogue involves both: the attempt to appreciate the other tradition for its own sake *and* to appropriate something of that tradition without losing touch with one's own.

But if an interest in world religions needs no justification, inter-faith dialogue does. What can it possibly mean to 'appropriate' something of another tradition? Does not Christianity teach that Christ is 'the way, and the truth, and the life'? What need is there to learn from other ways if the fullness of truth is revealed in one?

Such an attitude, however, brings with it the risk of a smug isolationism or – worse – a bigoted intolerance, the conviction that the highly complex issues raised by life in a pluralist society are born of 'their' refusal to see the truth, and are not 'our' responsibility at all. However we understand the deeply ingrained Christian motivation for mission, it cannot be reduced to the desire to save the 'infidels' from the darkness of their ignorance and sin. But neither can it be satisfied by the benevolent tolerance of the well-

2

motivated, sympathetic historian of religions. A succession of in-sights into the way that religion, culture and history interact may inform and stimulate reflection but may also turn into a piece of theological voyeurism. Inter-faith dialogue is more than usually enriching but it would be quite wrong to interpret this as a justifi-cation for Christians 'using' other faiths in order to supplement whatever is lacking in their own. Must there not be some element of criticism and questioning as well as mutual enrichment in the dialogue?

This book is not, however, a 'repetition with sundry examples' of what I wrote about in *Religions in Conversation* (London: SPCK; Nashville, TN: Abingdon, 1989), where I was concerned with the contemporary debate about the theology of religions and with the more theoretical questions about the relationship of faiths raised in the last paragraph. This book begins where the last one ended, with the implications of that question: What can Christians learn from other faiths? This is not an 'inter-faith theology' (should such a beast be possible), but a modest attempt to come to terms with the Christian experience of dialogue. What are its aims and its limits, its problems and its joys?

All dialogue is anchored in personal experience and is therefore limited. My main experience is of Buddhism, as a casual browse through these pages will show, and the main focus of dialogue is between Buddhism and Christianity. But Buddhism cannot be understood without reference to its Indian roots, any more than the gospel makes sense when separated from the traditions of the Judaism of the Hebrew Bible. If I have presumed to venture into Islam as well, it is not with the intention of providing an instant summary, still less a complete survey (for which I am not compe-tent), but in order to give a fuller account of the single Abrahamic tradition and to consider more fully some of the problems which the prophetic religions face. In the post-Rushdie world no book on inter-faith relations is complete without some reference to Islam.

Thus what I have written is no more than an introduction to some of the themes and ideas which one theologian-cum-student of religion thinks significant. I hope it will not come across as a sort of Cook's tour round the world religions – albeit informed with a few theological asides. If we remain content with inevitably vague generalizations, such as the Muslim's commitment to the tran-scendence of God or the Buddhist's meditative quest, we risk a distortion of our understanding of Islam and Buddhism. More

3

than that: in our enthusiasm to come to terms with the highly complex world of religions we may fail to recognize how much purely Christian concerns have dictated the agenda.

It would be nice if religions could be fitted into neat categories to aid the process of comparison, but even the great world faiths escape simple classification. Religions are different, so are the people who practise them, so are their expectations and the questions they ask. What makes for particular modes of religious motivation and behaviour is one of the major themes of this book. If Christians – or indeed any people of faith – are to learn from those whose beliefs and practices are different or 'other', then they need first to understand something of the cultural and historical context in which those differences were formed.

There is, however, another, and a more fundamental, point to be made. Each of the great religions has a certain *internal* coherence, a developed way of looking at and reflecting on human experience, which makes it unique. No particular aspect, a belief or a practice, makes sense without reference to the rest. In Christianity, for example, the incarnation implies the Trinity and vice versa; in Buddhism the doctrine of conditioned origination is the correlate of the teaching about 'no-self'. This, of course, makes the process of inter-faith dialogue and comparison more difficult, for we can never be sure that we have understood *the whole* of a particular teaching. However much we may learn there always seems to be more to be fitted into the total picture.

A certain level of generalization is necessary, of course, and there are bound to be points where my account of the total picture is inevitably limited and partial. I hope, however, that I have not risked too much distortion. Learning about another faith is somewhat akin to learning another language: not so much a matter of learning the different words but of entering into another world, full of idioms and imagery which interact and play on each other in a way which can never be translated adequately. I am always amazed at the way in which children seem able to learn different languages from an early age without getting them confused. Maybe the same thing happens when people learn about another faith: an alternative language develops, one which exists in many ways in parallel with one's mother tongue but which remains always 'other', almost but never quite a world apart.

This analogy may present us with a starting-point. In the following pages I want to show how at the heart of all religions there are certain patterns of belief and practice which establish communities of faith and give them a motivation for action in the world. Faith and spirituality are interlinked. My first concern will be with 'the spiritual' and contemporary experience of religion. Then I shall try to trace the outlines of a distinction often made between the Middle Eastern, prophetic religions, and the more mystical traditions of India. I shall try to show how faith is formed through ritual and myth and transmitted through canonical traditions and sacred scriptures. Using as a basis the models of spiritual practice which arise in India, I want to show how the different forms of prayer – liturgy, meditation and devotion – arise, and what they represent in terms of the religious quest.

The language of faith is not an esoteric language, reserved for the initiates, with little to say about everyday hopes and fears. If people of faith are to speak to one another, and – more important – if they are to speak to the world, then the language which they use must be capable of engaging with, and responding to, everyday experience. Thus the quest for human perfection or salvation and the relationship between prayer and action form an important part of this account. Finally, some attention must be given specifically to the language which is used to describe the final goal and justification of the religious quest: the Divine Mystery itself, what in the West we call with easy casualness 'God' and in the East by a whole variety of terms.

CHAPTER 1
Spirituality and the Spiritual

Take heed that you are not led astray; for many will come in my name, saying, 'I am he!', and, 'The time is at hand!' Do not go after them. And when you hear of wars and tumults, do not be terrified; for this must first take place, but the end will not be at once.

(Luke 21.8–9)

Predictions of the imminent revival of religion are almost as frequent as predictions of its imminent demise. In practice nothing is ever so simple. Idly glancing through a recent survey of social and cultural trends, I came across the following portentous judgement: 'In periods of massive social change, the depth of religious experience exceeds organized religion's capacity to invoke it.'[1] The authors predict that by the end of the current decade we will be witnessing a huge revival of religion in all parts of the world. Whether we think of the resurgence of fundamentalism, the vogue for New Age movements, or the never-ending fascination of the activist West with the contemplative calm of the Orient, there are signs everywhere, they say, that the insecurities provoked by a century of world wars, nuclear holocaust, racial genocide and impending ecological disaster have brought with them a new millenarianism. Given the significance of the date, the year 2000, it would be surprising if that were not the case, but religion in the popular imagination means a number of different things. What sort of a religious revival are we talking about?

At the outset we would do well to distinguish between a thirst for the 'spiritual' and a genuine growth of interest in the great world faiths. With the obvious exception of Islam, indications of a new ferment of activity in the traditional forms of religion are difficult to detect. The decidedly ambiguous phrase, 'the depth of religious experience' refers to something which is happening on the margins of 'organized religion', among people who have lost faith in the ancient traditions. This points to something which is surely more significant than the prospect of a millenarian expan-

6

sion. What we are witnessing is a shift in understanding of the nature of religion and the role it is expected to play in people's lives. It is not that religion has suddenly become acceptable again; rather one particularly seductive way of thinking about religion has begun to find a niche in the lives of – some – people in the First World.

Here religion has been removed from the public domain and, following the trend of the times, has been privatized. We are forever hearing that people still believe in God, that such and such a percentage admit that they have been influenced by some indescribable presence or power. Yet the signs are that organized religious practice is dwindling, that most people would no more think of going to church on Sunday than they would consider voting for a local fringe party in a general election.

We can distinguish two popular perceptions of religion: the ancient traditions which are for the few, and the purely personal beliefs and the all but non-existent practice of the many. According to this latter perception religious faith is expected to present people with answers to 'spiritual' questions which, almost by definition, are quite separate from the political and social spheres. It is this version of religion which this book sets out to challenge.

Faith and the Faiths

Of course, the dichotomy is considerably more complex than I have allowed, but I am not writing a social survey. This is not the place for analysis, still less for apportioning blame. My point is that faith and a fascination with the 'spiritual' are not the same thing, however intimately they may be connected. This book is about faith, that almost indefinable attitude which expects to find ultimate truth in the experience of a sometimes hostile and distinctly unsatisfactory world; but it is also about *the faiths* – which are not just collections of individuals searching for personal meaning but *communities* formed by faith.

The great world religions have all too often been seen as rivals for people's allegiance, alternative versions of the meaning-giving activity which is faith. Signs of the exclusivity which has long characterized inter-faith relations are still very much alive, as the furore over Salman Rushdie's *The Satanic Verses* has shown. Far from representing a simple clash between Western post-Christian liberalism and the intransigence of a still medieval theocracy, the

7

'Rushdie affair' shows what a complicated phenomenon religious faith really is. I shall have occasion to return to this theme later. At this stage let us note that tolerance and sympathy sometimes go hand in hand with very strained relationships. One does not have to probe deeply to find prejudice and suspicion mixed in with what is often a very slow growth of understanding. Such differences and disagreements need to be appreciated just as much as those mercifully harmonious moments of peace and tranquillity when people of faith know that they do share far more than keeps them apart – or can be put into words. Deeply held beliefs and passionate convictions are not to be changed overnight. Nor should we expect them to be. However much these communities of faith may have learned in the last few decades to come closer together in co-operation and mutual support, they will always test the limits of the other's imagination and question each other by the mere fact of their strangeness.

This needs to be said loudly. The prediction with which I began conjures up a picture of a great department store in which alternative brands of 'coping mechanisms' and 'identity structures' are available to the interested consumer – commodities, like a suit of clothes, which can be discarded or changed at will. The 'spiritual' version of religion conveniently forgets that, sooner or later, some extremely difficult questions have to be asked: about what religions are, about what it is to be 'truly human', about how faith enables people to speak of what is most sacred and precious in their lives – not to mention even more intractable questions about truth and falsity. Glib talk about a revival of interest in religion obscures the real issues which inter-faith dialogue raises and, what is worse, brings with it a potentially damaging way of thinking about the very function and role of religious faith in human living.

'The end will not be at once'

In the secularized West very personal beliefs may be fashionable, but communal or organized practice is not. It is fine to believe in God – provided God accepts the place assigned. To acknowledge such a split (present, to some extent, in all of us) is only being honest; to accept it uncritically may be disastrous. For in its train come other dichotomies: splitting private experience from social, immediate concerns from global, the world of 'the spiritual' from the world of politics. At one level, for instance, there is the sort of body–soul dualism which has bedeviled Christian asceticism for centuries. At another we find an even more insidious tendency to turn religion into an exercise in the practice of resignation and detachment. A literal 'other-worldliness' devalues life in this world. Heaven and earth are set up as rivals. The Kingdom of God which Jesus proclaimed is turned into a reward for a life well spent in this 'vale of tears'.

That there is truth in these dichotomies is obvious. People suffer and die; there is no perfection or fulfilment this side of the grave. Jesus announced that the 'Kingdom of God is among you' (Luke 17:21, JB), but he also said that the final judgement is 'not yet', that the good wheat and the tares would grow together until the harvest separated them at the end of time. Such realism informs all religions. Buddhism, as much as Christianity, teaches people to accept that – in the final words of the Buddha – 'all compounded things are subject to decay'. The very name of Islam means 'submission', acknowledging the sovereignty of Allah, the compassionate and merciful. Hinduism is dominated by the concepts of *karma* and *samsara*, the round of rebirths, the result of past action, which must be patiently endured in this fateful *Kali-yuga*, the age of decay. And yet to acknowledge and live with the dichotomy is one thing; to accept it as *absolute*, the final fact of existence is another. Eventually all dichotomies will be overcome. The question is *when*. At the end of time? Or does the end begin *now* – with all sorts of implications for our understanding of the human condition?

Religions have very different answers to these questions and a whole spectrum of opinion could no doubt be constructed. Concepts of the human good, images of the Divine, visions of the person, all vary – sometimes in a quite bewildering fashion. Some religions stress the social element in the expression of faith; others tend to the individual and personal. Nevertheless, all religions are concerned, in some sense, with making people whole, with what Christians call salvation. All look forward to an ultimate reconciliation, not division. An acknowledgement of sin, suffering and distance goes hand in hand with hope in an eventual greater harmony. A Christian's belief in God, a Buddhist's striving for *nirvana*, a Muslim's concern to do the will of Allah, have this much in common. The means of achieving that reconciliation differ – and differ enormously. But, while religions have to live with the dichotomies and dualisms mentioned above, they are never accepted as the final word on what it means to be human. It is highly doubtful whether any of the great world faiths would buy our other-worldly 'privatized' version of religion.

Religion: Private Belief or Public Concern?

Faith, then, is the heart of religion, and faith is not to be reduced to a particular type of 'spiritual' experience. Faith aims to unite the sacred and the profane in everyday life, not keep them rigidly separate. Predictions of a new millenarianism suggest that there is a growing interest in things religious. But is this to be understood in narrow terms as a pursuit of some sort of private 'spiritual' experience, or as a genuine interest in the wisdom contained in the traditional teachings of the great world faiths? Today's religious millenarian seems to be opting for the former. This is what one would expect. Western culture has lost much of its sense of identity. If it has an identity it can only be characterized as post-Christian, based at best on the typical liberal consensus that religion is concerned with the strictly sacred or spiritual; at worst on a sort of residual loyalty to a few private rituals, a mixture of nostalgia and superstition.

The latter attitude needs no commentary, and it would be tedious to trace the roots of the former. Suffice it for the moment to quote the well-known definition of religion given by William James, the celebrated American psychologist and pragmatist philosopher. James talks about religion as 'the feelings, acts and experiences of men in their solitude, so far as they apprehend themselves to stand in relation to whatever they may consider the divine'.[2] The privatization of religion seems to have been in full swing at the beginning of the century. It is difficult to ignore the concentration on subjectivity and the failure to give any attention to the way religions are formed and grow in a social context. And yet, as popular opinion has affirmed James' definition, the academic world has gone in a different direction. Contemporary religious studies gives as much attention to anthropological and sociological considerations in the formation of religious traditions as to questions arising from textual and historical study. It is recognized that, before religions are systems of ideas, they are communities – groups of people – bound together by faith in an ancient tradition. Faith is not a private but a very public affair.

It is to be hoped that the thirst for personal experience can be met by a deeper knowledge of what the religions themselves have to offer. To put the best interpretation on the 'new millenarianism', what we are witnessing can be understood as a search for genuinely spiritual values. Clearly this is to be welcomed. The greed which is inseparable from the enterprise culture, the damage which decades of ruthless exploitation have caused to the environment, the famines, feuds and communal violence which daily assault our TV screens, are not just signs of human limitation and sinfulness. They all show how far we fall short of realizing the noblest of humanist values – liberty, equality, the pursuit of happiness – let alone achieving anything which can remotely be regarded as leading to that deeper harmony, a sense of ultimate purpose or destiny, to which the great religious traditions of the world aspire. The danger is that, if we are not careful, we find we have uncritically accepted an understanding of 'religion' as 'privatized experience' which simply does not measure up to what the religions actually say.

The Religions Themselves

Can the religions themselves, not some sort of 'spiritualized extract', respond to the spiritual hunger which so characterizes this millenarian age? My intention is to consider some major themes which will contribute to a human, though not a humanist, spirituality; that is to say, one which rejects a dualism of sacred and secular, which seeks the Divine in this world rather than pines for it in another, and which holds out the possibility that the transformation promised at the end of time may, in some small way, be already present, affecting people here and now. Only if the wisdom of the great religions can contribute to the search for religious experience will these dichotomies be bridged. My quotation from the *Megatrends* survey suggested that religious experience often exceeds the capacity of 'organized religion' to invoke it. Perhaps, but the contrary thesis may turn out to be more significant: in times of upheaval and cultural disorientation the human search for meaning springs from – and eventually returns to – the traditional wisdom of the great religions of the world.

11

Any tendency to treat the religions with less than complete seriousness, still less to dismiss them, is to be avoided. Today's encounter of religions is highly complex. What is to be learned from it? In the first place, lived experience – what people actually *do* when confronted with the mystery of the Divine – is often more significant than theory and theology. As a Hindu lawyer once said to me – with a smile – 'I am not interested in what you have to say about God; I want to know what God says about you.' In the East religion is an issue, a natural part of people's everyday lives. Piety and prayer are no more reserved to the privacy of the home than worship is reduced to a sentimental attachment to the two great feasts of the Christian calendar. In Britain inter-faith dialogue takes place – if it takes place at all – in the pages of our more enlightened newspapers or in university common rooms; in India I would be more likely to find myself discussing religion in a busy advocate's office or while buying fruit in the local bazaar. The public vitality of religion is obvious to anyone who has taken time away from the tourist trails.

It is, however, very easy to lament the demise of much traditional religious culture and to contrast Eastern spirituality with Western materialism. Such comparisons are often unhelpful, to say the least. Much of the lure of the 'mystic East' has arisen from the craving for novelty, from the mistaken conviction that in the West religion – at least as it is presented in its institutional forms – no longer has the power to console and challenge. It is only right, however, to point out that Hinduism and Buddhism have no monopoly on prayer, meditation and God. The most fruitful inter-faith conversations are those which bring to light not the insights of the other but the forgotten or undervalued aspects of one's own tradition. For a Christian the question which I raised in the Introduction – What can we learn from other faiths? – must lead, sooner or later, to a reflection on the roots of Christian faith. As well as giving to the other, the dialogue enables those willing to take the risk to receive back.

Inter-faith Spirituality

My initial contention is that we must avoid an approach to 'spirituality' which drives a wedge between the spiritual and the social and thus makes it impossible for religious values to play a full part in the complex process of becoming fully human.

What, then, do we mean by spirituality? At its simplest spirituality is the practice of faith. All religions have some place for myth, ritual, meditation, mysticism, devotion and social action – all of which are ways of coping with the fundamental human desire to come to terms with the ultimate mystery of existence. Such basic practical attitudes are expressions of the fundamental conviction at the heart of all religion, that life ultimately makes sense. In this sense spirituality is prior to the great world religions as they actually exist. If faith informs practice, then practice establishes the communities of faith.

The faith which forms such communities is enormously powerful. This power is expressed not just in the intellectual coherence of a system, nor in some mysterious hold over the imagination which somehow supports people in times of crisis, but in the way a religion can motivate people to challenge and change the structures, both personal and institutional, of their lives. In the day-to-day life of a religious community liturgy, ritual and myth come first; doctrines, creeds and theology second. To argue for the value of religion on the basis of the latter alone implies that religions are like philosophies. They may appeal to the head and make for a good late-night argument when friends are ready for a game of verbal fisticuffs, but few religious founders – certainly neither Christ nor Buddha – would recognize what passes for religious feeling, let alone commitment, in smoke-filled pubs and common rooms.

What makes for a religious commitment? Theologians talk about the 'leap of faith', and no doubt there are many for whom commitment comes at the end of a long and largely intellectual search. Many more, however, commit themselves to the creed of a particular faith because they have first managed to identify with a church or community or group of people who meet together for prayer and worship. The symbols of faith, the celebrations and the social cohesion which mark the group have an authority which impresses itself on people, a power which makes them feel 'at home'. Commitment comes when the heart, not just the head, feels right. Spirituality is a way of expressing this commitment of the heart.

To put it another way, all spirituality is about the right ordering and challenging of the deepest of human desires. Whether we think in terms of the first disciples seeking out Jesus at the beginning of John's Gospel or of the many questioners who came to the

Buddha to have their doubts settled, spirituality begins with a movement of searching. All religions express this movement through different forms of prayer. These are the means to the end, ways of getting disordered desires and emotions under control. To that extent all spiritualities consist of an asceticism, a methodical structure of practices against which progress can be measured, as well as a clear vision or ideal to which actual practice is orientated. The problem is always to get a balance of the two. Discipline alone can kill the spirit, while the best of intentions, if unchecked, can be vapid or perhaps positively destructive. Spiritualities are differentiated both by their vision of the goal of the spiritual life and by the relative emphasis which they put on various practices, the way they seek to order the movement towards the desired goal. The 'commitment of the heart' comes with the resolution of this tension between vision and asceticism.

In their different ways, the spiritual practices which make up the great religious traditions are somehow able to integrate desire, enthusiasm and a mass of more uncontrolled emotions into a personally ordered whole. How this is done will always remain an infinitely mysterious process. The incredible variety of spiritual practices by which human beings struggle to bring meaning into their lives should put us on our guard against the temptation to make facile comparisons. The total submission to the oneness of God demanded by Islam is not to be married with the contemplative quality of the Buddhist *śunyata*, the 'emptiness' of things, any more than the ecstasy of the Sufi dancing dervishes is to be assimilated to the charismatic movement so popular today in many Christian churches.

The great religions are those which have developed and managed to maintain forms of spirituality which have a certain authority, a capacity to evoke a life-giving response in the hearts of people – or, to put it in a particularly Christian way, to be channels of God's grace. That authority must always be respected for what it is – if faith, in its many manifestations, is to be understood.

Living with the Questions

To begin our inter-faith dialogue here – with the authority of traditional practice – is to seek to avoid the largely intractable arguments which arise from more theological comparative exercises.

Very often it seems that what people do to express and practise their religion is different from what they *say* they believe. Thus a distinction can be made between spirituality and doctrine.

How are they related? In general we can say that spiritualities express beliefs but are not meant to be definitive of those beliefs. They are often very personal, representing a particular vision of the way that the great truths of faith harmonize together. To put it another way, they describe the way in which Divine Mystery is at work in space and time in the hearts of particular people. Doctrine presents us with the touchstone or rule of orthodox belief which not so much exercises a control over spiritualities or forms of religious practice as gives them a certain unity or coherence.

To be more precise, we need to note that the relationship between doctrine and spirituality varies from religion to religion. Some religions possess a strong doctrinal sense; others do not. No religion has produced more varied forms of spirituality than Christianity, with its pilgrimage centres, its sets of devotions, innumerable spiritual movements and different types of religious order, each with an appropriate vision of the way the gospel message should be lived. The fact that excesses have often been condemned along with more celebrated doctrinal 'isms' never seems to have dampened the spiritual imagination. But that is hardly surprising in a religion which bases itself on the doctrine that God has appeared in human flesh. Islam, on the other hand, is quite uncompromising in its condemnation of what it sees as the Christian tendency to anthropomorphize God. Accordingly we find in Islam a much simpler code of practice, based on the five pillars and reflecting the Qur'anic principles of the oneness and sovereignty of Allah, but it would be wrong to caricature Muslim spirituality as formal and legalistic; Islam too has its mystics and a rich tradition of devotional literature.

The religions of India present a different picture. Hinduism, arising out of the richness of Vedic religion, with its hymns and speculations about our knowledge (and lack of knowledge) of the Divine, might almost be described as a set of spiritualities in search of an organizing doctrine. It may be true that orthodoxy is not a Hindu concern; none the less, we should not ignore so many dominant principles, from the monistic teaching of the Vedanta to the honoured position held by gods like Krishna, Rama and Mahadevi, the goddess, which give Hinduism a recognizable form.

15

For many people the attraction of Buddhism is that it allows for so many different forms of practice, from the simple taking of the refuges (see p. 114–15), to the imaginative meditations of the Vajrayana and the silent sitting of Zen. Yet no religion is so strong about the special characteristics which set it apart from its Hindu parent: the doctrine of 'no-self', the law of conditioned origination and the sometimes baffling but none the less consistent teaching about the ultimate *nirvana*. In Buddhism the principle of 'skilful means' – the ability to adapt practice to purpose – follows from the principles enunciated in the Noble Eightfold Path, particularly Right View; only the enlightened teacher can instruct others.

It would be possible, but unhelpful, to speculate about the myriad ways in which the practice of a religion relates to the fundamental principles of faith. Rather, I want at this stage to emphasize that spiritualities do not answer questions but give people something which they can *do* in order to live with the unanswerable. Each spirituality is unique; usually each one emerges from the particular experiences of certain figures – mystics, prophets, holy men and women. Their insight into the religious tradition and consequent capacity to cope with their own lives draws out and releases something new from the tradition which enlightens the lives of others. Thus each spirituality changes the way we see doctrines affecting people's lives, providing a practical way of living with questions.

Forms of Spirituality: Learning from the East

It is not, however, as if the particular forms of spirituality which we find in the different religions are the exclusive property of particular religions; it is not as if Hinduism is based on one, typically Hindu, form of prayer and Christianity on another, typically Christian, one. One religion may, in fact, contain a number of different forms and there may be more similarities *between* different religions at certain points than *within* the same religion. Buddhism, though often characterized as a religion of mysticism, has a rich devotional tradition. How the two fit together often seems a bit of a mystery, but one could equally ask of Christianity: How does the monastic religion of the desert fathers express the same faith as the extreme devotionalism now being manifested at Medjugorje?

When we look at the religions of India we find there a wide variety of spiritual practices, ranging from complex liturgy to the simplest and most personal of devotions. The term which is often used to describe the different forms of Indian spirituality is *yoga* (a word which gives us 'yoke' in English) or *marga*, a word meaning simply 'way'. Both words have the connotation of practice. To compare Indian spirituality with Christian is to note in the first place that the former does not so much ask how one knows something as how one should *act* in order to know. Thus *yoga* or *marga* should be understood as 'spiritual exercise' or spirituality.

In Indian religion forms of practice are usually grouped under three heads, three different spiritualities: *karma*, work, *jñana*, knowledge, and *bhakti*, devotion. For the Hindu these three ways sum up a vast number of *sadhanas* or particular spiritual practices. Each stands on its own as a form of prayer and spiritual practice valid in its own right. Each is an attempt to live with the dichotomies described at the beginning of the chapter or, more properly, with the inevitable ambiguities which surround the mystery of the transcendent which is yet immanent, the 'totally other' which is yet the very core of our being. To that extent there is no difference between the three. They all emphasize one aspect of the divine-human relationship and develop ways of recognizing and responding to Divine Mystery. Just as in Christianity there are different forms of mysticism – the lonely contemplation of John of the Cross contrasting with the more apostolic following of Christ typical of Ignatius of Loyola – so in Hinduism the ritualistic *puja* of the devotee, offering flowers before the divine image, contrasts with the ecstatic singing of devotional hymns by pilgrims seeking *darshan*, a vision of the god at some great centre. Different practices for different people at different times.

However, the well-known Hindu *trimarga*, the 'three ways', is more than just a useful summary, a multicoloured religious umbrella for covering – and relativizing, as Hinduism tends always to do – all the religious practices of humankind. It is also instructive about the process people go through when attempting to come to terms with their humanness. Each practice represents a particular stage in that process. Equivalents can be found in all faiths. This takes us back to where we began, with the contemporary concern for the 'spiritual'. A properly balanced spirituality will only come about if attention is paid to all forms of spiritual practice, not just to one exalted at the expense of the others. How this balance is developed and maintained is, perhaps, the most important thing that Christians can learn from the experience of other faiths.

Notes

1 John Naisbitt and Patricia Aburdene, *Megatrends* (London: Sidgwick & Jackson, 1990), p. 255.
2 William James, *The Varieties of Religious Experience* (New York and London: Longmans, Green & Co., 1902), p. 31.

CHAPTER 2
The Religions and God

God is the light of the heavens and the earth. His light may be compared to a niche that enshrines a lamp, the lamp within a crystal of star-like brilliance. It is lit from a blessed olive-tree neither eastern nor western. Its very oil would almost shine forth, though no fire touched it. Light upon light; God guides to His light whom He will. God speaks in metaphors to men. God has knowledge of all things.

(Qur'an, sura 24)

While the origin of the divine light in the world is, in the words of the Qur'an, 'neither eastern nor western', the metaphors with which God speaks necessarily are. There are the religions: great world-encompassing traditions like Christianity, Buddhism and Islam, more specifically culture-bound creeds, such as Judaism, Sikhism and Hinduism, a vast assortment of primal and animistic religions, local creeds and ancient tribal cults, and an increasing number of new religious movements, some with syncretistic roots in the past, many sprung from the imagination and energy of one charismatic individual. Looked at purely from the student's angle religions are, in a very obvious way, human phenomena, as worthy of study as geography or mathematics or any other subject of human endeavour. As social realities they represent structures for coping with life. At the heart of all religions, for instance, are stories – myths, legends, records of the founder, deeds of saints. By putting themselves in touch with the past people can find the inspiration they need to deal with the present and look to the future. Yet not all metaphors are equally useful; some ways of speaking of God are misleading and some positively destructive.

The Power of Religion

All spiritual practice, festivals, ritual, cult and devotion, is based on the conviction that people's experiences of this world point to something superior or beyond, some invisible force or power. The

19

wilder excesses of religion – Muslims reducing the Jihad to terror-
ism, Hindus enduring the pain of spikes and hooks in honour of
their god – may confuse and disgust the Western mind. But, if
nothing else, they remind us that there is much more to religion
than social convention. Part of the mystery – and fascination – of
religion is its power to motivate. Religions sustain and destroy.
They can help people through the most extraordinary personal
suffering; they can equally inspire the most dreadful barbarism.
Which is only to say that people's vision of the invisible, the beyond, or God, has an extraordinary power over them – a creative
and a destructive power. What people believe about the Ultimate
has an effect on their lives beyond integrating them into a particular culture; religion changes lives and makes people want to change
the lives of others.

Perhaps the most awkward question facing the supposedly secularized West is the relationship between religion and society. In
Britain we have inherited a complex philosophical and religious
sub-culture. Buffeted by post-Enlightenment liberalism on the
one hand and a renascent Islam on the other, traditional forms of
Christian faith find themselves caught in a dilemma. Should
Christian faith be a way of supporting the ancient tradition, a celebration of all that is best in society and a reinforcement of the culture, or should it represent the voice of criticism, a protest speaking
in favour of a different vision – a prophetic vision of the ultimate
demands which God imposes? Starkly put like this, the horns of
the dilemma may seem like extremes which enforce a painful
choice when they really represent equally important values which
have to be held together. Both must be maintained, but how? Since
the Reformation, Christianity in Britain has tried, with some
degree of success, to combine an established church with a
venerable recusant tradition which includes Roman Catholics as
well as Baptists and Presbyterians. Today Christianity in Britain
and in the West in general is part of a pluralist society. Today's
recusants are agnostics and fundamentalists; Christians have to
learn to tolerate and to question both. The same applies to people
of other faiths. Is it possible to build a society in which so many
religions exist? In brief: If we recognize in all faiths both a creative
and a destructive side, can the strengths of religious faith be
harnessed for the welfare of the whole without the exclusivist
element causing more friction than any society can be expected to
absorb?

Going Beyond Names

If the religions only presented different ways of integrating people into society there would be no problem. What complicates matters is that religions have very different visions of what is meant by society, about what it means to be human, and in what the human good consists. And yet if religions did not try to speak about what is of ultimate value, Christianity and Islam, Buddhism and Hinduism, would be no more than fatuous exercises in wish-fulfilment, games of make-believe. This much at least they have in common: a sense of what is of ultimate significance, even if the languages and the symbols which are employed are so diverse. The name may vary in different religions and cultures: Allah, Yahweh, Śiva, Vishnu. Names may come and go: the history of religions is full of dead gods, witness to the insatiable human appetite to understand and even control the darkest and most incomprehensible mystery of human life. Names may be consciously by-passed in reaction against the excesses of the human imagination, being replaced by an impersonal concept, like the untranslatable Hindu *Brahman* – or the Buddhist *śunyata*, 'emptiness'. The Hebrew Bible refuses to use the name of God, preferring the title Lord; the Upanishads deny the very possibility of naming the Ultimate, saying simply *'neti, neti'*, 'not so, not so'; Muslims go to the opposite extreme and present ninety-nine of the most beautiful names of Allah. All seek to speak of – or to show the limits of speech about – what is of ultimate value.

Not even Buddhism is atheistic – in the sense of denying any possible fulfilment to the deepest of human hopes and aspirations. If Buddhism is the exception to all the rules, then it is also the exception which proves the rule, which develops – and checks – that sense of the Ultimate not by denying human hope but by moving people in directions where they would rather not go. Buddhism is not just a very different example of religious faith, the conviction of ultimate value, but raises a very real question mark over our futile attempts to make the Ultimate, the Transcendent or God an object of study.

So much – little enough, perhaps – religions have in common. Religions, however, are manifestly different: whether we are thinking of beliefs about ultimate destiny or attitudes to human society, to say religions are all talking about the 'same thing' begs far too many questions. To make any comparison of religions as they actually exist can be an enormously confusing business. It would take no time to come up with a whole string of resemblances: the cultic, the experiential, the devotional, the ethical, the mystical, and many more. It can be done because religions do not exist in isolation but maintain some sort of continuity with each other. If they did not they would cease to be human phenomena. Beyond this largely superficial level, however, religions are unique in their practice and in the effect they have in people's lives. Islam with its *Shari'a* law exercises an extraordinary control over every aspect of social life. The structures of Hinduism, by contrast, are fluid to the point of non-existence. Buddhism, which began life as a development of the mystical side of Hinduism, asks for a free and personal commitment; the only authority is the internal restraint exercised by the teaching, the *dharma*. These, of course, are only impressions. In practice contradictions abound: it would be a melancholy act to concentrate on the destructive side, to list the crimes which have been committed in the name of religion. Is it, perhaps, a fruitless task to seek out any common ground or space where religions can meet?

The mistake, of course, is to talk of religions as if they are institutions of cult and law when they are more properly the beliefs and acts of ordinary people. If there is a coherence to be found in the way different people react to the mystery of the Divine it is not just to be discerned in what the canonical texts and creeds say but in what at any particular time people *take them* to be saying. To repeat: We cannot study God, only what people say about God and what they do to acknowledge the central importance of God in their lives.

It is obvious that for people of faith to understand themselves – let alone each other – a great deal of time and effort needs to go into investigating their origins and sources of motivation. Such is the necessary task of scholarship and academic analysis. It is less obvious how the tradition is to be made personal: the way of life of people rather than an academic abstraction. But it can be done. An inter-faith service in which I was involved focused on the rainbow as an image of harmony. In a sense the rainbow is neutral: each colour has its own connotations for the different faiths, and thus some very different ideas allow for some very divergent interpretations. Yet at the heart of them all is the knowledge that the sum total of the colours of the spectrum make up the single white – an assurance, as it were, of ultimate harmony. Other examples could be given – examples of the way people of faith can come together to support each other, to listen and to learn. The practice of inter-faith dialogue, still more the experience of silent time shared in prayer and meditation, builds the space in which the sense of the Divine can flourish and grow. Objective study and personal ex-perience coexist; the more that is learned about the faiths, the more faith grows.

The Mystical and the Prophetic

There are only three genuine 'world' religions: Buddhism, Chris-tianity and Islam. All three can claim a universal reference; all three have inspired extraordinary movements of missionary ex-pansion. Yet there are enormous differences between them. Buddhism is only one of the many religions which have arisen in the sub-continent of India, while Christianity and Islam share a common origin in the Jewish revelation. On the one hand, a reli-gion which originates in *yoga* and a personal quest for salvation; on the other, a strong and assured monotheism which demands com-mitment and response. It is almost as if we are speaking of two 'styles', or two 'types', of religion. Thus Indian religions like Buddhism and the early forms of Hinduism from which it sprang are often called mystical; the semitic religions of the Middle East are referred to as prophetic.

In general terms the distinction is helpful. Judaism, Christianity and Islam have a certain 'family resemblance'. They originated in the same part of the world and are all – in the Muslim phrase – 'reli-gions of the book'. Religions which recognize the presence of the Transcendent in the mystery of language – God as the one who communicates himself – are dominated by solitary, God-haunted, charismatic individuals, the agents of God's word. Hinduism and Buddhism, on the other hand, have a much more ambivalent atti-tude to the Divine, mainly, I suspect, because they are prepared to understand the mode of God's self-revelation in much broader terms. Thus the Hindu pantheon includes the wrathful Kali as well as the benign, fun-loving Krishna. A profound sense of Divine Mystery pervading all human activity – the dark as well as the light – is typical of the Indian attitude to the world. Christians, on the other hand, find the central focus of their faith in God the Father of Jesus Christ. Muslims deny the fatherhood of God but still speak of the oneness and sovereignty of Allah dominating the life of the community and demanding *islam* – submission. The mono-theism of semitic religion begins with the creator God who gives value to all human life. Buddhism and Hinduism, by contrast, ac-cept a vast pantheon of *devas*, gods, and innumerable denizens of the spirit-world, all of whom are a familiar part of the world of human beings. The 'jealous' God of Abraham, Isaac and Jacob is a far cry from the ten *avatars* or incarnations of Vishnu or the com-passionate Amitabha, the Buddha of the Pure Land.

In what sense are Indian religions 'mystical'? The search for equivalents is always a risky business. Hinduism does not boast of prophets in the sense of the Hebrew spokesmen for God. The mouthpiece of the ancient tradition is to be found in the priestly or *brahmin* caste, whose members are charged with preserving ancient values, the rituals and practices which make up the religion of the Veda. There is, however, another type of value and another type of religious practitioner at the heart of Indian religion. This is the *sannyasi*, the renouncer or wandering holy man, whose tradi-tional function is the recognition of the many ways in which the Di-vine is forever revealing itself in the world. The Buddha is only the most celebrated example. Today *sannyasis* are to be found living in temples and ashrams or simply wandering through towns and villages. For ordinary people they are tangible signs of the presence of the Divine and therefore objects of deep respect. They are no more prophets than the *brahmins*, but in religious terms they fulfil some of the functions of prophecy within the Indian traditions, notably in the way they point to the all-encompassing demands of God in their lives. Fundamentally, however, they are concerned less to proclaim God's word as revealed in the past, more to listen for the myriad ways in which the Divine may be heard here and now.

This distinction between prophetic and mystical religion may do something to overcome a temptation which is peculiarly Chris-tian – though not by any means the exclusive property of that tradi-tion. The God of the Bible, still more the God of the Qur'an, makes his will known – sometimes with great clarity. Prophets for the cause have never been lacking, prophets whose zeal and clarity of purpose has often degenerated into a bombastic dogmatism which has done scant justice to its origins in Divine Mystery. Hesi-tation in providing answers has rarely been a Christian failing. Buddhism, on the other hand, still manages to maintain the healthy reticence of its founder. Even today a Buddhist monk may not preach unless specifically invited. Buddhism has been called by various names – a philosophy, a way of life, a pessimistic world-view. For its critics it is either a sophisticated version of the worst aspects of Eastern nihilism or an amalgam of superstitious poly-theistic 'popular' religion – or both. But for the vast majority of Buddhists the *dharma*, the teaching of the Buddha, and the devo-tions and practices which have evolved over the course of more than two and a half thousand years provide support and strength, a vision both of the way things are and of the way things could be.

Thus it is with all religions, prophetic or mystical. Where does the difference lie? Partly in a sort of prophetic or mystical mode of operating – a way of presenting what is known; partly in the relative weight given to aspects of what is known. But, in the end, I suspect that the real difference lies in practice: a matter of *how* we come to know what is known.

Faith and Knowledge

In shifting attention from God, the Ultimate Reality, to the reli-gions we find ourselves dealing with languages – sometimes very different languages – capable of expressing this basic human sense of the Divine. What is it that holds these very different faiths together? If people did not have some awareness that their lives must *ultimately* make sense, some conviction that they *know* the Ultimate, God, their beliefs and practices would, no doubt, justify the strictures of the cynics and sceptics that religions are no more than examples of the human capacity for projection – and there-fore self- deception. There is plenty of both in much that passes for religious belief and practice today. Faith, however, is not a sort of blinkered obscurantism; it is founded on the conviction that human affairs are not meaningless, that, as Paul puts it, 'in every-thing God works for good with those who love him' (Rom. 8.28). Despite experience to the contrary, people go on believing, for such is the nature of religion. Even those religious men and women who have suffered most acutely the seeming absence of God, through personal loss or tragedy, still remain convinced that God remains. Religions, whether prophetic or mystical, help people to face what is often called simply the problem of evil. They may not provide answers – of an intellectual kind; they do help people to live with questions.

Thus to say that we 'know' God is only half the story. Whatever the strength of our convictions we have to live with the inevitable assaults which are made on the harmony and order of our world. Buddhists do not have a monopoly on systematic doubt. Mystics of all religions speak in negative terms of the impossibility of knowing the Ultimate, yet never for one moment consider giving up the desire to do so. Speech is often derided as inadequate – 'he who knows does not speak, he who speaks does not know' – yet the conviction remains that it is possible to speak about the Divine in the language of the religions. Prophetic religion stresses our desire – and capacity – to speak of God; mystical religion warns us of the limits of any language. What can it mean to speak of that which is acknowledged to be beyond words? What sense does it make to say that we 'know' God?

Christianity in common with the other 'religions of the book' starts with revelation. We do not know God; rather God knows us. We wait upon the divine initiative: God makes God known. The Bible is full of visions in which patriarchs, prophets and judges are confronted by a Yahweh whose demands cannot be ignored. The most famous conversion story in the New Testament depicts an illumination so violent that the persecutor Saul is left blinded – yet in no doubt about who has been speaking to him. Islam sees itself in the same tradition. The Qur'an revealed to the prophet Muhammad is the final and definitive act in a long process; the Qur'an is the perfect revelation of the will of Allah. Again God takes the initiative.

But Islam raises in an acute form the dilemma which must be faced by all prophetic religion: *Where* is the Word of God? What is loosely called fundamentalism has an easy answer – the inerrant word of scripture to which we respond with a passive obedience. Such a way of understanding revelation, as a purely gratuitous act, does scant justice to the Judaeo–Christian tradition. How many Old Testament prophets greeted the word of Yahweh with extreme reluctance? Jonah may be something of a caricature of the runaway prophet, but the story is still instructive about the struggle which *God* has to go through in order that God's will may be done. Thus when Christian theologians try to work out the precise relationship between the human and divine elements in the process they are doing no more than articulating further the basic convictions mentioned above: we cannot know God yet we are convinced that God has already made God known. The Christian debate focuses on the relative merits of the Bible and natural theology as sources of knowledge of God. Protestants begin with the former; Catholics tend naturally to the latter. The question is about how far our knowledge of God can be said to be continuous with our knowledge of the world. To what extent can one know God through God's effects? Or are we so totally blind that we have no hope of knowing God unless God takes the initiative – in the person of Jesus Christ? In the fourth gospel Jesus says that 'You did not choose me, but I chose you' (John 15.16) and describes himself as the one who points the way to the Father. Paul, no doubt reflecting on the violence of his own conversion, can say to the Romans that 'we do not know how to pray as we ought' (Rom. 8.26). It is the Spirit, praying in our weakness, who raises our hearts and minds to God.

Ways of Knowing

According to the strict interpretation of a prophetic tradition like Christianity or Islam only the divinely inspired revelation can give true knowledge of God. When we move to the East and to the religions of India we find the same questions being asked but given a different emphasis. More attention is focused on the various modes of human knowing or, to be more precise, on the ways in which the divine–human relationship may be expressed.

In Indian religion and philosophy there are usually reckoned to be four means of gaining valid knowledge: perception or experience, inference, comparison and testimony. The first and the last are the most significant. When we say we 'know' something we usually mean that we have had some personal experience of it or that we have been taught or told about it by someone else. More often than not the two go together: the best teachers are those who can encourage their pupils to learn from their own experience. In Hinduism there is an inherited tradition of wisdom, arising from the Vedic hymns, which is handed down from *guru* to pupil. The relationship is illustrated by the philosophical texts, the Upanishads, where we meet sages like Uddalaka who tries to instruct the young man Śvetaketu in the nature of Ultimate Reality. Any number of illustrations are used to bring home the truth contained in that most powerful of all the 'great sayings' of the Vedanta: *'tat tvam asi'*, 'That you are'. As the salt is lost in but still pervades the water, as the seed gives birth to the tree, so the great power behind the one reality we perceive and the heart or essence of the human person are ultimately one and the same.

But to speak this truth is one thing, to realize it for oneself is quite another. The Buddha too instructed his disciples in *dharma*, the truth about what is real, but insisted that it must become part of oneself – not just taken on trust but made fully one's own. The Buddha does not enlighten anyone; that his followers must do for themselves. The teacher's task is to point the way. In his last recorded words he says to the assembled company of monks: 'All compounded things are subject to decay; work out your salvation with diligence.' In matters pertaining to religious truth, testimony, what is heard, must go together with perception, what is experienced.

Perhaps I can explain what I mean with an example. In the Pali Canon of the Theravada school there is a famous sermon about the experience of *nirvana*. One monk asks another whether 'apart from belief, apart from inclination, hearing, argument as to method, from reflection on and approval of opinion, have you as your very own the knowledge that the ceasing of becoming is *nirvana*?' The monk replies that he has indeed experienced this truth of *nirvana*. Another monk confesses that he has not; he has, he says, *seen* the truth and understood it but he has not made 'bodily contact' with *nirvana*:

> 'Friend, it is just as if there were in the jungle-path a well, and neither rope nor drawer of water. And a man should come by, foredone with heat, far gone with heat, weary, trembling, athirst. He should look down into the well. Verily in him would be the knowledge – Water! – yet would he not be in a position to touch it. Even so, friend, I have well seen by right insight as it really is that the ceasing of becoming is *nirvana*, and yet I am not an enlightened one for whom all hindrances have ceased.' (*Samyutta Nikaya*, 2.115)

There is a distinction to be noted between the purely intellectual view or understanding of the truth and the personal experience of the truth in which full clarity, without impediments, has been achieved. This distinction runs right through all Indian religion and, in many ways, is the key to understanding the various forms of gnostic spirituality in the Hindu and Buddhist traditions.

The truth, whether taught by the texts of the ancient tradition or in the one-to-one contact between pupil and guru, is something which has to be internalized and experienced for oneself.

The problem is the same in all religions; how are we to be sure that we 'know' the Ultimate? In Christianity – and rather more so in Islam – the answer comes from God: a definitive statement given to particular persons for a particular purpose. This is the privileged tradition, God's own word, spoken to the people of the covenant. Christians are those who go on bearing that tradition for others; they will always want to confess that they only know God in and through the life, death and resurrection of that Word, Jesus Christ.

If in the Indian mystical tradition the emphasis is on personal realization, in Christianity the primary means of knowledge is not experience but testimony or revelation. However, this cannot mean we are to take the word of scripture on trust, as if the answer to the problem of knowledge is just to read the book. Any scriptural tradition has to ask how the text is to be read; in Christian terms, how *the Word* is to be discerned among the many words. The problem does not go away because Christians accept an external authority. Rather it becomes that of learning to recognize the way in which the mystery of Christ, the Word spoken by the Father, is made present. In Christ is found the 'pattern' of God's revealing love, but Christians still have to judge where and how that love is encountered. Revelation and experience have to be held together in all religions, even if the balance between the two is different from that found in Hinduism and Buddhism.

To draw a neat distinction between an authoritative revelation 'from above' and a more personal experience 'from below', however, rather misses the point. In all religions both are necessary and the differences are mainly matters of emphasis. Islam takes its stand on the former but not all Muslims fit the caricature of the fanatic fundamentalist eager to preserve the least flourish of the Qur'anic text. Buddhism insists on the latter but it does not follow that there is only one valid interpretation of the Middle Way which must lead to a solitary stoical indifference. The distinctions which we make in our spectrum of faiths are never absolute. Christianity is described as authoritarian and devotional, Buddhism as anti-dogmatic and mystical. And yet when we look at religions as they actually exist we find that such general descriptions very rarely fit. A Sufi sheikh I met once told me how much he had learned from meditating with his friend, a Theravada monk. One of the most prayerful experiences I have ever had was in the home of a Hindu in South India, chanting *bhajans*, devotional hymns, with a group of friends. Many Christians have gained deeper insights into their own tradition through the practice of Zen. Examples could, of course, be multiplied.

To sum up: I have tried to show that, when we look at the religions of the world, we find different answers to a single question: How do we know and speak of what is Ultimate? Prophetic or revealed religion runs the risk of appearing almost too self-assured. It needs a healthy dose of mystical reticence to avoid the charge of dogmatism. It is never enough simply to assert that 'I know God', for God can never be an object of knowledge in the way that things, ideas or concepts can be said to be known. God or Ultimate Reality can be 'known' only through the experience of faith: hence the different spiritualities or ways of religious practice which have developed to take people on the journey of faith as the mystery of Ultimate Reality unfolds itself. In revealed religion faith has the character of a response to God's initiative; in mystical religion faith is more like a search, a longing for the deepest meaning or value at the heart of *all* experience. But the difference between the two is more a matter of degree than of kind; the three types of spirituality which I outlined at the end of the last chapter, and to which we must now turn in more detail, all develop a particular way of knowing and speaking of God – and thus becoming more human.

CHAPTER 3

The Awakening of Faith

Now as he journeyed he approached Damascus, and suddenly a light from heaven flashed about him. And he fell to the ground and heard a voice saying to him, 'Saul, Saul, why do you persecute me?' And he said 'Who are you, Lord?' And he said, 'I am Jesus, whom you are persecuting.'

(Acts 9.3–5)

How does the journey of faith begin? Few have had the sort of classic 'Damascus road experience' which knocked Paul off his horse. The movement towards religious commitment is utterly mysterious. Most people find themselves confronted with a choice, whether or not to cross a new threshold, to share in the religious world of a community. Once there they find themselves learning a new language, not just words and phrases but symbols and images which enable them to articulate their conviction that the world of which they are part is ultimately and infinitely meaningful. To take such a step is, of course, very difficult. Before moving into what at first appears to be an alien environment, most people are apprehensive. The invitation to faith is nothing less than an invitation to change one's identity, or – which can be equally frightening – to find it.

Christians will insist that the invitation to faith comes from God; it is a supernatural gift beyond human power to grasp. The faith of Hindus is based on the Veda, the ancient texts which were 'heard' by the sages, a primeval Word spoken before time began. Even for a Buddhist a certain attitude of faith is required in order to hear the *dharma*, the word of truth taught by a Buddha, a truly enlightened one. But in each case faith is mediated through a religious community. The role of the community is crucial: in what it does and in the way it behaves it bears witness to what it believes. In external ritual and through the effect that the different forms of spirituality have on interior life, faith becomes an almost tangible reality. If a religion has authority it stems immediately from what is seen to be done rather than from creeds and statements.

Faith finds expression in the acceptance of the authority which characterizes a religious community. To understand the source of this authority is to recognize the power vested in the symbol or sign which points the way. The exuberant decoration of the Hindu temple is in marked contrast to the classical restraint of the Muslim mosque. Outwardly two religions could scarcely be more different. Both, however, recognize the need for those sometimes tiny and unremarked words, rituals and images which somehow manage to get to the heart of faith. To call them shorthand forms is not to diminish their importance. The Muslim *shahada*, 'There is no God but God and Muhammad is his prophet', the icon of Christ of the Orthodox Christian, the Buddhist *stupa* or burial-mound, may seem very different, but they have this much is common: each in its own way invites faith, leading people across the threshold of strangeness and into the presence of the Divine.

The Priority of Ritual

Both prophetic and mystical religions alike begin with the awakening of faith through the use of certain dominant symbols. For a Christian, of course, this means Christ, that person in whom God makes his invitation to faith. The earliest confession of faith of the Christian community seems to have been 'Jesus is Lord', but the New Testament is full of titles which express the conviction that 'in Christ God was reconciling the world to himself' (2 Cor. 5.19). When Jesus is called Lord or Christ or Son of God, the early Church is saying something about the way that God is acting in their midst and, therefore, about what God is like. For Christians God is there in the pain and suffering of the man Jesus, the one who fulfils the ancient prophecies of Isaiah about the suffering servant. 'He was despised and rejected by men: a man of sorrows, and acquainted with grief... Surely he has borne our griefs and carried our sorrows; yet we esteemed him stricken, smitten by God, and afflicted... The Lord has laid on him the iniquity of us all' (Isa. 53.3–6).

There is something quite extraordinary about the idea of a God who chooses to speak to a particular people, still more about a God who reveals himself in a man crucified as a criminal. That Christians have gone on proclaiming such a God in the midst of persecution and misunderstanding speaks volumes for the zeal of their missionary spirit, but much more for the inherent power of the story they have told and the images which they have used. In Christ is revealed the God of the 'poor in spirit', the 'meek', the 'pure in heart', and 'those who are persecuted for righteousness' sake'. To those who put their trust in such a God belongs the Kingdom of heaven, the 'pearl of great price' for which one will give up everything. Centuries of evangelism, preaching the God who suffers on behalf of others, have exercised an extraordinary power over the hearts and minds of humankind.

All this is true: the crucifix says more than many a weighty theological tome. But we still need to ask how such symbols exercise their appeal, how they inspire faith. A dispassionate assessment of Christian missionary activity must admit a good deal of failure. For every convert in Asia and Africa there have been scores who have listened and gone their own way. There are, of course, a number of issues here, among them the whole question of appropriate missionary strategy and the question of the adaptation of the gospel message to local needs – a point to which I will return shortly. More immediately I want to ask: How are the symbols of faith to be used if faith is to be encouraged and developed? The point I want to make is that faith only comes alive when it is actually seen at work in the life of a community, most especially in the rituals which celebrate the identity of the community.

In ritual and worship ancient memories are celebrated and thereby made present again. A sense of continuity with certain foundational events which give an identity to a community is established. The celebration of the Jewish Passover is only the most obvious example – an event which continues to inspire not only Jews who gather every year to recall what is 'special about this night' but Christians too who remember the night on which 'Christ our Passover was sacrificed'. Divali for Hindus – the feast of lights, the New Year festival – Id al Fitr for Muslims – the feast which celebrates the end of the fasting month of Ramadan – are further examples of festivals which gather people together and establish them in the present: the tangible, easily recognizable forms which religions assume.

The point can be illustrated further from Indian religion. Even in the tolerant relativist world of Hinduism a certain priority must be given to ritual. The religion of the Vedas is highly formal, a complicated structure of chanted hymns and elaborate ceremony in which everything has its place. If there is an authority in Hinduism it rests with the Veda, a timeless *dharma* or Sacred Truth revealed to the ancient seers. This is the bedrock of the tradition, from which everything else in the luxuriant world of the Hindu grows. In Hinduism, and – I would contend – in all religions, liturgy or ritual has a leading or guiding function. For most people religious practice begins not with some particular religious experience but with the acquisition of a language which enables them to interpret their experience – *all* their experience, not just holy feelings or a sense of the mysterious. The language is learned from the people who speak it and from the symbols which express faith – in short from ritual, liturgy and story, in the calling to mind of the great images and symbols of the tradition. It is only subsequently that they are reinforced through personal meditation and developed into a personal devotion, a sense of being loved by God.

Ritual and Sacrifice

The word used in Hinduism to refer to the spirituality of ritual is *karma*, literally work or act. It implies that there is something to be done, that spiritual practice is a human activity demanding time and effort. But the action is also divine, the work very much a form of *co*-operation. The original sense behind the word *karma* is the work of the Vedic sacrifice – not so much the activity that must go into the complex business of building the altar and preparing the offering, but the action which the sacrifice represents.

There are various theories to account for the origins, and therefore the meaning, of sacrifice. Some would explain it as a gift to the gods either to bribe them or as an expression of homage or dependence; others go for an expiation theory or one which emphasizes the social element, gathering the community around the sacred meal. It is often difficult to judge between them. It may be that the origins of this most basic of all religious acts are lost in the mists of time. What is clear, however, is that we are dealing with a way – or, to be more precise, many different ways – of recognizing or formalizing the relationship which exists between the human and the Divine. The word means to make something sacred; the 'something' mediates the Divine to the religious community. In other words

34

sacrifice is a formal act or ritual which uses the objects of this world to put people in touch with what is of ultimate value.

The language of sacrifice is very much at the heart of Christianity. Indeed it would be difficult to understand Christianity without some reference to the expiatory sacrifices of the Old Testament or the suffering servant and Son of Man motifs which the Old gives to the New as interpretations of the meaning of Christ. Sacrificial thinking is at the heart of the Eucharist, the ritual which is formative of the Church, the community which gathers in the name of Christ. The Eucharist is not just a reliving of the Passover and the Last Supper, but also a 'giving thanks' for Christ's self-sacrifice. Given the highly complex symbolism associated with the Eucharist it is not surprising that Christian theologians of various denominations have found here a happy hunting-ground for speculation and controversy, but it is all too easy to lose track of some important sacrificial concepts. Suffice it to mention the covenant, sealed in blood, which is applied by Christ to his own death in the institution narratives (e.g. Matt. 26.28), and the way in which Paul speaks of the Eucharist as a sacrificial banquet: 'The cup of blessing which we bless, is it not a participation in the blood of Christ? The bread which we break, is it not a participation in the body of Christ?' (1 Cor. 10.16).

And yet the very term sacrifice presents us with problems. The word conjures up a whole world of unfortunate connotations, from the literal, but distant and nowadays all but incomprehensible, bathing of the people of Israel in the blood of the covenant (Exod. 24.8), to the heavily spiritualized idea of 'giving up' something trivial during Lent in preparation for Easter. Is there nothing in between? It may well be that the insights provided by other faiths may help Christians to redress the balance somewhat and to rediscover the meaning of that fundamental religious act which expresses the human need to establish and maintain contact with the Divine.

The Vedic sacrifice focuses our attention on the mediating function of sacrificial – indeed of all religious – language. In the great Vedic rituals *brahmin*–priests were charged with the task of acting on behalf of the people in their relationship with the gods, the *devas*. The sacrifice was surrounded with an extraordinary mystique, so much so that it came to be regarded as essential to the maintenance of ordinary life. The 'work' of the sacrifice was the 'work' needed to keep the world in being; it was as if the great edifice of creation required regular 'propping up' or, to change the metaphor to something more appropriately Indian, the cycle of ages needed regular 'pushing forward'. *Karma-yoga*, then, is firstly the Vedic sacrifice; later it comes to apply to all forms of ritual or liturgy, from great public performances, such as the dedication of a temple, to the humble offerings made before the image of the deity in the corner of the family home. But the key point to note is that *karma-yoga* is a work of co-operation: by developing correct *heavenly* relationships humans and gods *together* keep the universe in being. Thus *karma-yoga* is extended to the everyday social sphere as well: correct relationships with one's fellow creatures are just as important as relationships with the gods.

The fact that the *brahmins* were the only ones who knew the sacred lore and therefore could negotiate that dangerous area where sacred and profane interacted gave them enormous power, a power which could easily be abused. This is not the place to explore the story of the degeneration of the great Vedic sacrifices into magic and superstition. Enough to note that religiously the complex acts of the various priests failed to satisfy those in whose name the rites were performed. Other examples could be cited. The rubrics which so much dominated the old tridentine Latin Mass, for instance, produced an object of great aesthetic beauty which, nevertheless, too easily became an end in itself. The ancient Vedic sacrifice seems to have been in a class of its own when it comes to an obsession with form and rules. But, just as the Latin Mass needed reform if the true purpose of liturgy was to be maintained, by a much lengthier and more painful process the Vedic rituals, for all their beauty, have gradually given way to simpler acts of worship which appeal more directly to the sense of identity of the people. The lesson is simple: in any religion, a concentration on form rather than meaning, hedging the central acts about with all sorts of peripheral actions, must eventually produce a stultifying effect. People need more from ritual than a vague sense that the professional practitioners are up to something mysterious and 'holy'.

Identifying the Sacred

That, perhaps, is the first lesson to be learned from Indian tradition of *karma-yoga*. Another is more positive: the way that ritual enables us to name or identify the sacred. Today the great Vedic sacrifices are no more. Their spirit continues, not in great formal gatherings, but in the myriads of tiny rituals which surround the life of the average Hindu. Like all liturgical acts, they are performed as markers and signposts put down to remind others of who *this* people is and what it holds as important. Washing in the sacred waters, formal prostration before the image of the deity, the offering of flowers and rice, are all acts of prayer. The fact that they are also very public acts does not seem to detract from the spirit of intimate devotion which they express. But the greatest contemporary example of *karma-yoga* is undoubtedly the pilgrimage – the public act of worship *par excellence* which points quite specifically to the realm of the sacred in everyday life.

The focus of pilgrimage is, of course, the temple or shrine, the end of the journey. This may be associated with some event of local significance, legendary or mythological. Many of the temples of South India, for instance, celebrate stories associated with local gods and goddesses. In making the pilgrimage people are reminded of these all-important events and through the use of devotional songs and chants relive the influence they have on their lives. To that extent pilgrimage is much the same in any religion: a liturgy full of devotion which unites a group of people in a common purpose.

Hindu temples, great and small, are nothing if not centres of pilgrimage. Pilgrims may be seeking *darshan*, 'sight' of the deity who dwells in the sanctuary, and may show devotion through *puja*, acts of reverence and respect. Clearly what they *do*, their individual liturgies, are expressive of a deep faith in the power of the deity to answer their particular needs, but it is not just what goes on inside the temple precinct which is significant. I shall be examining the spirituality of devotion in a later chapter; here I want to focus on the religious meaning of pilgrimage, the journey to the sacred site.

Liturgy, as we have already noted, is a formal communal act which supports and develops a sense of the Divine. To see the Hindu temple as the gathering place where pilgrims perform their individual devotions rather misses the point. Rather, a relationship is established between the pilgrim and the temple itself. The temple building, as much as the act of pilgrimage, serves to concentrate the attention on the god who dwells not just at the heart of the temple but in the heart of the worshipper.

The building is sacred for the obvious reason that it houses a sacred image. In the great temples, however, the architecture, decoration and general environment are used very deliberately to enhance that sense of the sacred. Pilgrimage can be an arduous activity, involving great hardship and penance; a sense of anticipation is built up over days and weeks of measured walking, accompanied by the chanting of devotional hymns, as the pilgrim moves towards the centre of the temple, the darkened chamber known as the *garbhagriha* or 'womb house'. The very word evokes a sense of the single divine principle from which the whole of creation, including the pilgrim, can be said to grow. Thus the sanctuary represents nothing less than the heart of the universe in which the solitary pilgrim must find his or her place. With the great temples, their towers beckoning across the plain, this significance is obvious. Not that all temples are gigantic structures which seem to engulf whole cities. There are hundreds and thousands of tiny shrines in every corner of the land, some of them no more than a few stones set by the road. To the pilgrim, whether involved in a formal act which may take weeks or simply pausing for a moment before a wayside shrine, they act as reminders of the divine presence which is inseparable from the land and the people.

The Interior Pilgrimage

In Hinduism, however, and to a lesser extent in Buddhism, there is also a cosmic significance to the act. The object is to enter into the heart, to realize the truth that dwells within. To that extent the real pilgrimage is an internal one. The temple is not the home of the god, still less a meeting-place for the faithful, but the centre of the universe, the point from which life comes and to which it returns. The pilgrim is following the gift of life back to its source.

Thus it is not just that the temple points to an event and evokes a memory. The temple is itself a sign of the coming together of all things. When pilgrims enter the temple they are returning to the cosmic harmony from which they came. Among the rock-cut temples of Ellora in Maharashtra, up in the Western Ghats, many miles east of Bombay, is the enormous monolith Kailasa dedicated to Śiva. A temple hewn out of the mountain speaks of God at the heart of the world, from whom all life comes, as a river flowing down to the sea. Pilgrimage, that simplest of all human liturgies, represents the human return to God, the reintegration of the Many into the One.

The first and most important lesson to be learned from the spirituality known as *karma-yoga* is that it represents a highly developed awareness that the Divine is present within the world. Theological subtleties about God being both transcendent and immanent seem inappropriate. God is immediate. God is present in and through the land. Images of riverbanks dotted with temples, hills festooned with *stupas*, mountains crowned with pagodas, spring to mind. Romantic images, no doubt, but indicative that for so many people the Ultimate is not distant but a reality which they experience at the heart of their world.

The Indian mind does not see the 'theological problem' of the interaction of divine and human in the same way as Christians do. Christians start with a concept of God provided by revelation; everything else, human beings, the world we inhabit, other creatures, all are made thoroughly subordinate to the single Divine Reality, their Creator and Master.

In India people *begin* with an awareness of the Divine already pervading all living things. That everything which exists should be One is not a controversial point; the difficulty is over the nature of the Many, the multiplicity which makes up this world and the variety of sentient beings it contains. The Christian sees all things telling forth the glory of God, but, as God's creation and God's gift, sees that they are to be *used* for the glory of God. The Indian has no less a sense of divine gift but is much more conscious that the Divine Mystery *is* the gift. For the Indian mind it is a question of seeing *into* the world, not beyond it.

The second point follows from this. The visible world as we experience it veils the invisible – not just the spirits, the gods and other beings whom we cannot see, but the One reality which preserves them all in order or harmony, the one *dharma*. Everyone has a particular task or way, a *sadhana* – the word means something like 'purposive quest' – which must be practised in order to search out and see the Divine, the One which is yet Many. Both Hinduism and Buddhism are thoroughly relativist when it comes to practice. In Mahayana Buddhism it is the particular skill of the *bodhisattva*, the compassionate teacher, to find ways of leading others to enlightenment. For the wise teacher, who knows the Truth, all spiritual practices can be used if the Divine is immediate, for there is no such thing as the profane. Thus, while it seems correct to give to *karma-yoga* a certain priority in so far as it celebrates the key symbols and thus preserves the tradition, it will, in

39

practice, be reinforced by other spiritualities. The only question is what is appropriate for *this* particular individual.

Maintaining the Tradition

Later chapters in this book will look at aspects of the three forms of spirituality such as the place of sacred texts, mystical and devotional prayer, before taking up the question of the relationship of prayer and action in the wider sense, moral and social activity in the world. There is, however, one last aspect of the spirituality of liturgical prayer which needs brief consideration. The fact that ritual depends on the re-enactment of traditional symbolic forms is its strength, but – used exclusively and dogmatically – it can also be a weakness.

I have spoken of *karma-yoga* as that practice which develops and sustains faith by leading people 'over the threshold' into a new experience – in the case of pilgrimage, literally so. But it is clearly possible for images, however famous and revered, to lose their aura of authority. First-century Palestine is not twentieth-century Britain; the world of sowers and shepherds, deserts and vineyards, is no longer familiar. An enormous effort of intellect and imagination is needed to bridge a cultural gap nearly two thousand years wide. And facing today's international Church is an even bigger cultural divide: first-century Palestine is not twentieth-century India. A religion which claims an absolute authority for certain events and particular icons of the Divine has to learn to interpret them in contemporary terms.

'Inculturation', the answer of the Church to this challenge, has become something of a buzz-word. Yesterday's insight can become today's jargon – and consequently be ignored. Yet all that is being emphasized is a universal truth: that the presentation of faith has to be adapted to particular cultural circumstances. The meaning of the key symbols of faith is not always obvious; it will be unlocked by the demands of each context.

It is not only traditional Christianity which has to come to terms with culture. The furore over the publication of Salman Rushdie's *The Satanic Verses* is only the most recent example of what happens when the beliefs of a revealed religion clash with the intellectual world of the modern secular state where reason is the only authority. To dismiss the Muslim community's reaction to Rushdie's book as the last vestige of religious obscurantism, a tedious relic of pre-Enlightenment times, is to show little awareness of the real issues. Whatever the indications to the contrary, religions are neither monolithic structures with answers for every eventuality nor private spiritual visions of the world intended to console the world-weary. They help people to identify themselves in a sometimes strange and godless environment. Religious icons, whether the figure of Christ or the text of the holy Qur'an, cannot be sneered at without causing deep hurt to the communities who hold them dear. That said, the hostility which condemns the humanist values of the secular state as at best moral equivocation and at worst the work of the devil is not likely to enhance that identity but only to destroy itself by intensifying feelings of anger and despair. At some point religions have to make the effort to become credible to the society of which they are part. Failure to do so means turning faith into credulity and spirituality into superstition.

Any dialogue between faith and unbelief causes tension and strain. No one should ever expect the practice of faith to be easy. But religions which have survived the blasphemies and insults of centuries (usually from each other) are unlikely to lose their sense of identity because the modern world does not want to know. Faith – to repeat – is based on the conviction that human affairs are not meaningless; it is not a ready-made database providing instant answers. A creative dialogue which genuinely seeks for meaning and truth, whether with other religious believers or with society at large, enhances rather than destroys faith by focusing attention on the key symbols which sum up and express a religious identity.

Building up Religious Identity

This returns us to the heart of the problem: What is it that maintains religious identity? Sometimes the dialogue with society is accepted as a necessary evil – no more than an opportunity to put one's case to the godless. More often than not the apologetic crusade is left to one side; theologians debate about the relative merits of forms of words and try to present the ancient tradition in a way which is both faithful to the past and a reasoned answer to the questions of the present. So much of moral theology, for instance, develops in this way, especially where there is no clear argument to be adduced from scripture. There is obviously an important place for such a dialogue; the channels of communication between Church and world have to be kept open. But, in a society which is as confused about the role of religion as it is obsessed by economic performance, such exchanges have to be supplemented by something else.

This something is faith, the search for meaning. In this chapter I have tried to explain the role that ritual plays in the awakening of faith. Through formal acts of worship the symbols of faith come alive, leading people from the exterior pilgrimage of form to the interior pilgrimage of knowledge and love. While there is clearly more to religion than ritual, there is no religion *without* ritual – even if by this is meant only the remembrance and celebration of identity. The problem is *ritualism*. Rituals tend by their very nature to be exclusive; a Christian may cross the threshold of a Hindu temple or a Sikh *gurdwara* but will not be able to participate in the ceremonies performed there. This is not to say, however, that there is nothing to be learned from being present at the rituals of another faith community. Apart from the obvious point that Christians may very well learn how much they share in common with others, faith supports faith. Experiencing faith at work, as it were, is literally edifying, building up faith and making it credible. In doing so, it is to be hoped that the dialogue may do one thing more: familiarity with the other means breaking down the bounds of exclusivity, reminding us that there are other forms of spirituality and other ways of expressing religious identity.

CHAPTER 4
Sacred Words and Sacred Texts

'Hear, O Israel: The Lord our God is one Lord; and you shall love the Lord your God with all your heart, and with all your soul, and with all your might. And these words which I command you this day shall be upon your heart, and you shall teach them diligently to your children, and shall talk of them when you sit in your house, and when you walk by the way, and when you lie down, and when you rise.'

(Deut. 6.4–7)

Rituals support and celebrate symbols, but where do the symbols of faith come from? Very often they are to be found at the heart of sacred texts which, in some way, are authoritative for a particular tradition. According to the standard proclamation which accompanies the sacred texts read at Christian services, what has just been read is divine revelation, the 'Word of the Lord'. However, the very ease with which the average Sunday congregation mechanically repeats 'Thanks be to God' should give pause for thought. Quite possibly the scripture reading was a piece of highly chauvinist tribal history or the sometimes testy comments of a recently converted Pharisee on the local problems of a first-century Christian community. Of course, not all of the Old Testament, still less Paul, is obscure. Passages of rare beauty appear side by side with some parochial and highly unchristian polemics, but even the gospels set curses alongside beatitudes and the slaughter of the innocents next door to the birth of Christ. What relevance do such ancient texts have in this post-modern scientific age?

At the end of the last chapter I touched on the crucial issue of inculturation, the need to translate or adapt a tradition to ever-changing circumstances. Earlier I raised the question of how prophetic and mystical religion interact. Both questions are relevant here. All religions – not just Christianity – claim a privileged access to truth, whether it is understood in terms of a divine revelation or as a way to be followed by the initiated. Buddhists talk of taking refuge in the *dharma*, the teaching which is proclaimed by an enlightened one, just as Christians confess their faith in the 'Word of the Lord'. To the outsider it must sound as if faith is no more than a capacity to believe some thoroughly odd and incomprehensible stories and statements. Even to the insider faith appears at times to be blind and irrational. And yet, if faith really is the search for meaning, then the privileged status given to scripture and time-honoured traditions is very often the decisive factor in a complex process of seeking to understand. But in what sense 'decisive'? How does one justify the use of such authoritative statements?

More important: how do religious people avoid the sort of belligerent self-assurance which allows no criticism of authority? The so-called Rushdie affair has raised the spectre of 'fundamentalism' in religion – in Christianity as much as in Islam. This attitude which interprets all experience in terms of certain key statements of belief which are beyond criticism is at work in many parts of the world. How useful a term fundamentalism is may be open to debate; personally I find it too vague and general a concept – a 'media-word' which, used uncritically, serves only to obscure the important lesson which the phenomenon has to teach. I shall return to this point later. Suffice it to say for the moment that what has been happening in the Islamic world, where one constantly comes up against a fierce commitment to an inviolable tradition, demands that all people of faith examine the place they give to sacred words and sacred texts in their lives. Is it the literal word of God, as Muslims believe, which makes immediate and unarguable demands on us here and now, or just an ancient record which tells an ancient story – full of meaning for a people far distant from us in time and culture but no longer immediately relevant to the present generation? To ask the question less tendentiously: What part do we expect sacred texts to play in the life of a religious tradition, in its formation and growth?

Scripture as Liturgy

It is important at the outset to note a certain bias in Western culture which, rooted in Christianity with its emphasis on written texts, on creeds and theological statements, tends to be highly literate. This understanding of the nature of Christianity has had a marked effect on the way in which scholars have looked at the scriptures of other religions – and therefore I would suggest at the

Christian scriptures as well. The scientific study of religion which developed in the latter part of the nineteenth century expected other religions to reflect what was found in Christianity. Thus 'Comparative Religion', as it was called, sought parallels in theological themes, symbols and practices. But the agenda was set by Christianity, or – to be more precise – a particular view of Christianity.

Today we are more conscious of the way other faiths differ – sometimes quite fundamentally – from Christianity. Christians at worship will be celebrating the Eucharist, listening to the scriptures being read, or praying together with the minister or priest. Hindus, on the other hand, have a number of different ways of practising their faith. Religious practice has a community aspect in so far as pilgrimage and the many rituals which accompany temple worship demand the participation of the group. But more typical of Hinduism is the lone devotee or solitary holy man searching for the Eternal in the depths of his heart. How does a mystical religion use the hollowed traditions of the past?

The texts of the orthodox Hindu are known as *śruti*, 'what is heard', and consist of the Vedic hymns, the *Brahmanas*, commentaries which are to be used in the sacrifice, and the philosophical Upanishads, which are believed to contain the essence of Vedic teaching and are to be studied and meditated on in the heart. But in practice Hinduism often gives a more important place to 'secondary' traditions, sometimes very local and often unwritten. One of the first experiences I had of Indian religious culture was watching a drama danced by a *devadasi*, literally a 'servant of the god'. What impressed me most of all was the amount of communication which went on through the use of very exact and precise gestures. Moods are expressed in movement, sometimes only perceptible by the practised eye. There is, in the many different styles of Indian dance, a classical form which must be adhered to. People know the story before the dance begins; they know the outcome. The point is not to learn or experience something new but to join with the dancer in what is a celebration of the old and familiar.

At one level dance-drama is pure entertainment: ancient stories and myths are acted out for the benefit of an enthralled audience. But such drama is also a religious event in which actors and audience take part in an activity which has cosmic implications. The dance has a sort of sacramental quality. In the *Raslila*, for example, the stories about the cow-herds' infatuation with Krishna, the

45

dancers, who are often children, not only take the parts of the main characters, they somehow *become* them. One example which I watched began with the guru, the teacher of the troupe, actually making a solemn obeisance before the children who played Krishna and Radha. They were no longer children, but had become a manifestation of the Divine, making present the ancient story of the love of God for human beings.

What part do such performances play in the religious life of the people? The distinction I would want to make is between the purely informative function of religious texts and the liturgical. So much of any religion, as it is actually practised, depends not on the reading or study of texts but on a participation in the story which it represents. Stories such as the *Raslila* are an essential part of the fabric of Hinduism. There are, of course, classical versions of the central myths to be found in the great epics and the Puranas, the 'ancient tales' of the gods. But these enormous texts are simply compilations of a tradition which probably goes back to the earliest forms of Hindu folk-culture. The religious tradition depends on the constant re-enacting of ancient folk-memories, making them present again.

This is true of most religions, but let me stick with Hinduism for a while longer. What significance do the dancers have for the people watching the performance? Classical Hinduism depends for its coherence and continuity on the role played by the *brahmin*-priests as the head of the caste hierarchy; they maintain the traditions vested in *śruti*, the ancient hymns of the Veda and the philosophical texts known as Upanishads. But this is not the whole of Hinduism. The dance-rituals which are to be witnessed today represent very often the religion of low-caste village communities for whom the actors are, to all intents and purposes, fulfilling the role of priests; they, rather than the *brahmins*, are responsible for mediating the Divine to the people.

The fact that religion which is represented by the dance-drama does not depend on a written and spoken tradition means that we are dealing with an experience which is evoked by a *ritual act*. Through the careful enactment of the drama, representing an act of creation, destruction or liberation, the community lives out its most significant moments and memories. The stories about the gods become a present reality; Krishna, for example, holding up the mountain Govardhana to protect a village against the thunderbolts of Indra, becomes the protector of all those who recall his past exploits here and now. By starting with the community of persons whose fundamental religious acts attempt to establish a sense of identity, we find that scripture primarily has a *liturgical* purpose.

The Formal Structure of the Tradition

This may sound obvious but it is all too easily forgotten. Buddhism, for example, is often regarded, like Christianity, as a highly literate tradition in which sacred texts are used to maintain the orthodoxy of belief and practice. There is something in this, of course, but the ritual context and purpose of Buddhist scripture needs to be remembered. To go into a Buddhist temple or meditation hall is to be confronted by the Buddha himself – or at least by many statues and images of the Buddha which remind monk and lay person alike of the central truth of their religion: the enlightenment which Buddha achieved and promises. The many practices and devotions of the different schools of Buddhism centre round meditation but are no more limited to the selfish pursuit of an individual *nirvana* than Roman Catholicism begins and ends with Mariolatry. Even – and perhaps especially – meditation is a highly formal activity which requires careful attention not just to posture and breathing but also to the 'structure' of scripture recitation which puts it in its proper context.

On first acquaintance, however, the Buddhist scriptures seem a far cry from the Hindu dance-drama. Most people are impressed less by their liturgical form than by their sheer length. The Buddhist canon contains biography sermons, legend, history, philosophy, religious poetry and a lot else. It is quite vast. There is no single version: nor is it possible to extract an 'original core'. The Chinese canon would require more than half a million pages of print; even the relatively manageable Pali canon of the Theravada school runs to forty-five closely printed volumes. Sometimes one could wish that the Buddha's disciples had taken more seriously his call to avoid entering into scholastic arguments about abstruse metaphysical questions.

However, the very length and the formal structure of texts is the clue to their significance. Unlike the Qur'an or the Torah, which are accepted by Muslims and Jews as the revealed word of God, the 'Buddha-word' has a purely conventional and very practical function, that of enabling people to follow the Middle Way. Along with the disciplined life and the practice of meditation, study of the scriptures attributed to the Buddha and his enlightened followers is part of the way of life to be followed by all who would achieve *nirvana*. The essentials of Buddhist belief can be reduced to a very few formulae, such as the Four Noble Truths and the Eightfold Noble Path. Why then the massive expansions? In Buddhist terms words have no absolute value; in fact they may well be obstacles to true enlightenment. But at the *practical* level, where words are to be *used* for the end of attaining enlightenment, there is no reason why there should not be an infinite number of ways of expressing – that is to say helping people to understand – that truth.

To be a Buddhist is to take refuge in the three jewels – Buddha, *dharma* and Sangha. For our purposes the second is the most important: the Buddha's teaching. But it can only be understood by reference to the Sangha, the community which is the vehicle or means of its preservation, and the Buddha, the enlightened teacher. The word *dharma* comes from a root meaning to uphold or give substance to something; it is simply the Truth about Ultimate Reality. This idea, that *dharma* is something which is learned in the experience of enlightenment, is extremely important. The Buddha's *nirvana*, the experience of final release from suffering, is not the result of an exterior revelation, still less the invention of a religious genius. It is the realization of the Truth about Ultimate Reality which has existed for all ages but which a Buddha has discovered and preaches out of compassion to this world-age. This means that there is not just one Buddha but an infinite number, both past and future, and that everyone has the potential of Buddhahood – of discovering and preaching *dharma*.

Scripture and Revelation

For Buddhism, as for Hinduism, the truth taught by the scriptures is eternal, without beginning. The Buddha, like the *rishis* or seers of the Veda, *hears* the eternal truth; unlike them, the truth is ascertained through his own efforts at clearing away the personal obstructions which cloud human understanding. Other Buddhas have done this before him; others will repeat the process after him. But always it is the same *dharma* which is revealed. Now using the concept of revelation is appropriate so long as we recognize that what is being described is, in Buddhist terminology, *sambodhi*, enlightenment. The metaphor at work here is that of 'waking up', with its connotations of coming out of a semi-conscious dream state and seeing things as they really are. Such an experience is a revelation in the sense that a 'veil' is taken away from the object of consciousness. The Buddha, however, is not a 'revealer' in the same sense as Christ may be understood as the revelation of the Father. Buddha is a teacher but his role is to enable others to overcome the fog of ignorance which keeps them, as it were, in a dream state, and to help them realize their potential to become enlightened, to be Buddhas.

When Buddha lies dying his disciples ask who is to direct them when he is gone. The reply is simple: they are to be lamps to themselves, guided by no authority other than that of the *dharma* which he has preached to them. 'The truths and rules of the Order which I have set forth and laid down for you, let them, after I am gone, be the Teacher to you.' Ultimate authority, then, lies in the sermons and instructions which make up the canon of scripture.

However, Buddha also told his disciples that they could, if they wished, revoke the 'lesser and minor rules' of conduct. Unfortunately no one asked what these rules were. According to the tradition Ananda, Buddha's favourite disciple, was actually disciplined by the First Council for his failure to ask. Add to this the general point, already noted, that the disciples were – in the final words of Buddha – 'to work out their salvation with diligence', and you get a very real tension set up: between those who would safeguard every word and tradition as the exact Buddha-word from which no one is ever to deviate, and those who would see the Buddha-word in much more pragmatic terms, to be used or discarded as appropriate; in short a tension between conservatives and progressives.

This tension is at the heart of the major division in Buddhism, between the Theravada school, the 'doctrine of the elders', to be found today mainly in Śri Lanka and South East Asia, and the Mahayana, the 'great vehicle', which is dominant in Tibet, Mongolia, Korea, China and Japan. It is often said that the Theravada is élitist, dependent on a clear distinction between monk and lay, while the Mahayana is egalitarian, offering many ways of salvation open to all. Like most generalizations it contains a grain of truth. However, a more interesting point emerging from recent scholarship is a re-evaluation of the place of the scriptures in the Mahayana tradition. In brief: the Mahayana is a tradition based on reverence for 'new' revelations, the teachings of the Mahayana *sutras*.

How are such 'new' teachings to be justified? Basically it comes to this: the word of an enlightened disciple, one who has realized the potential of Buddhahood, is as valid a 'revelation' as the word of Siddhartha Gautama, the 'historical' Buddha. It is said that 'whatever is well-spoken' – that is, whatever conduces to progress on the way – is 'spoken by the Buddha'. The process by which the 'sage of the Śakyas', to give him his Mahayana title, became a god-like figure, to all intents and purposes the centre of a theistic devotional cult like Christianity, is long and complicated and ill-understood. But one of the key moves is the growing reverence which is shown not to the Buddha but to the actual texts which embody his teaching. To read anything of the Mahayana *sutras* is to notice the emphasis placed on the benefits which are to be gained from reciting even a few words. Sometimes it seems as if they have an almost magical significance, that the words themselves, and not what the words point to, are what count. Is this a shift in the direction of 'fundamentalism'?

There is, I think, something more profound at work. After the Buddha's death his memory was preserved for the monks in their adherence to the monastic discipline, which was given precise scriptural warrant in the *sutras*. For lay people, however, a different form of spirituality was developed: that of devotion to the physical relics of the Buddha interred in various *stupas* or burial mounds. Remembering the summary teaching of Buddhism as the Middle *Way* and the Noble Eightfold *Path*, we might say that lay people make the pilgrimage in a literal, physical sense, while the monks make it metaphorically through the 'internal' journey of meditation. With the Mahayana, attention shifts from devotion to the Buddha in his relics to devotion to the Buddha as he can be said to continue in another way, in the spoken and written word, in the book. For the Buddhist the text *is* the Buddha; it is through devotion to the Buddha in the *dharma* that one has access to the same profound spiritual experience as the 'author' of the book, that enlightened one who has discovered the eternal truth and passes it on to others out of compassion for their suffering.

To understand this we must note one thing more. The Mahayana *sutras* are to be recited out loud in order to create a certain devotional atmosphere. For the Western Christian mind the memorizing of a text is a practical means of preserving the tradition – a stage necessarily prior to the more reliable method of writing the material down. What we forget is the effect that the memorizing and recitation of sometimes enormous texts must have on the people who do the reciting. To repeat: sacred scriptures have their effect through being recited in a necessarily formal situation – a recitation which does not so much express the identity of the community as actually form it.

To read and study a text is to let oneself be guided by its directives; to listen to a familiar text being recited, still more to memorize it oneself, is a very different experience. The very 'style' of such memorized texts – their rhythms, repetitions and mnemonic lists, intended for public recitation rather than private study – has a psychological and spiritual purpose. It creates the atmosphere in which religious faith can flourish. The sound of the chant, the smell of incense, the physical movements and gestures, all combine with the familiarity of repetition to evoke a spontaneous response. The language of faith – but not just the language – forms religious consciousness. There is no doubt that the chant of Buddhist monks, regular and rhythmic, develops a certain inner concentration and stillness, whether the chant takes place before or after the period of meditation. By engaging the feelings and calming the emotions the oral word has a much more powerfully transforming effect than any amount of mere reading or study.

The Sacred Word

It may be that these ideas, admittedly taken from the mystical religions of India which subordinate the sacred text to the quest for insight and experience, will help us to come to terms with the perplexing problem of fundamentalism. This, as popularly understood, is to be found mainly, though by no means exclusively, in the prophetic religions of the Middle East. Does the distinction which I have tried to make, between the formative and informative functions of sacred texts, help us to understand what is happening in many religions today – perhaps especially in Islam?

Islam cannot be understood apart from the other faiths I have characterized as prophetic. The Hebrew greeting of *shalom*, God's gift of peace, is familiar; similarly the corresponding Arabic word *salaam*. The same semitic root gives us Islam and Muslim. The word means both peace and submission; a Muslim is one who enjoys God's gift of peace through having submitted to the sovereignty, the 'oneness' or *al-tawhid*, of God, Allah. The holy book of the Muslims, as everyone knows, is the Qur'an, a word which means both collection and reading. The first formal lecture I heard on Islam provided me with a complete analysis of the written text: the 114 suras or chapters, the 6,616 verses, the 77,934 words and so on. This somewhat exact and legalistic approach to the Qur'an, that which sees it in highly formal terms as defining the nature of the Umma, the Muslim community, can easily obscure the fact that Islam is no more monolithic than any other faith. There are many schools and many traditions of interpretation of the text. What they all share is a strong sense of the sanctity of the text – literally *God's word.*

In fact the Qur'an (as opposed to the *Shari'a*, the code of law) contains comparatively little legal material. The major themes concern the nature of the Godhead, a cosmology about the structure of the universe and an eschatology about final judgement and eternal life. All of this is set in a wider framework of the story of peoples, kings, prophets and saints through the ages. The background of a type of 'sacred history' speaks of the battle which goes on in each person to follow the one straight path set out by God, who rewards and punishes people according to their actions. The message is simple: life begins with God and eventually returns to him. Those who accept this truth by submitting to God earn the right to enjoy eternal life with him.

The revelation of Allah in the Qur'an is often seen as the fulfilment of ancient prophecy – a prophecy which goes back to Adam and Abraham and includes such figures as Yahya, John the Baptist, and Isa, or Jesus, and leads, of course, to God's final word, the Qur'an, dictated by the archangel Gabriel to the prophet Muhammad. There is an Arab story which likens human existence to a journey from oasis to oasis. The first stop is at an oasis called Moses, the second is called Jesus, the last is Muhammad. It is natural, therefore, to think in terms of a continuity from the Old to the New Testament and then to the Qur'an. However much truth there is in this idea, it is also quite misleading. If we restrict ourselves simply to Christianity and Islam, the correct parallel is not between the scriptures of the two traditions, nor between the central founder figures. The Word of God in Islam, the written word, is parallel to another Word, the *Logos* of John's Gospel. In the Qur'an the Word is made book; in Christianity the Word is made flesh. Jesus is the message; Muhammad the messenger of God's word, the mouthpiece through which God's will is made known to humanity.

This means that there is something intrinsically sacred about the recitation of the text and about its presentation in a written form. Qur'anic calligraphy is, of course, one of the artistic wonders of the world, but I am more concerned with the effect which the spoken word has on its hearers. A devout Muslim prays five times a day – the *Salat*, one of the five so-called 'pillars of Islam'. Each occasion of prayer takes place – ideally – in the mosque when the community lines up in ranks facing the *mihrab*, the niche which points in the direction of Mecca. It consists of ritual prostrations and certain formal prayers preceded by the *Fatiha*, the opening sura or chapter of the Qur'an.

> In the name of God, the Compassionate, the Merciful,
> Praise be to God, Lord of the Creation,
> The Compassionate, the Merciful,
> King of Judgement-Day!
> You alone we worship, and to you alone we pray for help.
> Guide us to the straight path
> The path of those whom You have favoured,
> Not of those who have incurred your wrath,
> Nor of those who have gone astray.

The power of the language cannot be overstated. Although vernacular translations of the Qur'an are allowed, in order that its prescriptions may be studied and known by all the people, its liturgical use demands the original Arabic; everyone is expected to know a certain minimum and to use it – for Muslims it is nothing less than the language of God.

There is no doubt that, read in translation, the Qur'an is heavy going – prosaic and at times incoherent. But in listening to Muslims expounding their faith I have been struck by the ease with which sometimes lengthy sentences trip off their lips in support of some truth or other. To some extent these are used as apologetic 'proof texts' to support an argument. There is, however, something else: for the devout Muslim the words are the very presence of God, a guarantee of his special care and compassion. One modern commentator calls it a 'divine magic'. Because the verses of the Qur'an are understood to have this special 'God-given' status, they are held to have a power which goes beyond anything which we might learn from them through the processes of reasoning, that is, through simply reading or studying them. Rather, in individual recitation, still more in hearing them recited by a whole congregation, the verses act like a sort of talisman which protects people. Thus even the physical presence of the Qur'an is held to have a sanctifying power, inspiring the same sort of reaction as the Blessed Sacrament in a Catholic. When a Muslim is in difficulty he or she will naturally turn to the Qur'an – *not* to find a 'message' of comfort, but to let the words themselves work their pacifying and comforting spell. In Islam there is precious little by way of religious art or symbolism and no iconography at all – beyond the words. In a mosque all you will see will be elaborate versions of the key sayings; on either side of the *mihrab* will be found two words only – Allah and Muhammad, reminding people of the *shahada*, the cornerstone of the faith: 'There is no God but God and Muhammad is his prophet'.

Coping with Fundamentalism

Despite the obvious differences in the three traditions I have discussed, they have this much in common: the very sound of the words being recited is religiously significant – more significant, in fact, than an understanding of the meaning of the words. In Islam, the recitation of the Qur'an is a ritual act, whether performed alone or with the whole congregation, as at the midday prayer on a Friday. Similarly in the very different devotional Hindu tradition, the dance-drama is the making present of a cosmic act in human terms. And in Mahayana Buddhism a certain atmosphere conducive to meditation is built up through the recitation of the sacred *sutras*. This, again, is obvious when we focus on the way in which the texts are *used*: in worship and ritual, as part of the formal process by which a community of faith identifies itself. Particular words and phrases, even whole passages, become familiar and develop a sense of security in which faith can flourish.

It is important, however, not to overstate the case. Not all religious texts find their origins and purpose in the ritual. Informative texts exist side by side with formative ones, even if the latter have a certain priority. The Hebrew Bible contains the books of the Law and the Prophets as well as the cultic Psalms; together with the *śruti* literature Hindus venerate *smriti*, 'that which is remembered', especially the *dharmaśastras*, legal textbooks. This in itself does not present a problem. Once a community has celebrated its identity it is natural for it *then* to look to ancient stories, records and traditions as a way of establishing and articulating itself. Practical questions, whether about prayer or the life of the community, are always going to be asked. The problem arises when the community finds its sense of identity under pressure from without – perhaps by another group celebrating a similar story in a similar way. At this point it may react to crisis by turning inward, making the formative traditions which were intended to produce *internal* harmony a force for attacking an *external* threat.

This, put very simply, is the dynamic behind the modern phenomenon of fundamentalism. The term began, of course, as the label of a movement within American Protestantism which, in the early decades of this century, felt threatened by evolutionary thinking. Today's Muslim fundamentalists seem more incensed by the religious nihilism of contemporary Western culture. But in both cases we are dealing with a type of thinking which is basically reactionary, in the literal sense, and expressed – as we are all too well aware – in great outpourings of anger and frustration. Not that fundamentalism itself is the cause. Anger is caused as much by a sense of inability to operate within the given internal structures as it is by an awareness of overwhelming force from without. To put it in psychological terms, insecurities are eventually projected outwards; in the case of militant Islam, on to the free-thinking Western unbeliever.

This may explain one important aspect of the fundamentalist phenomenon. What I have tried to show is that scriptural traditions have a primary role in the formation of a community. Naturally they will also assume a secondary, apologetic, role for the ordering of the community. However, once used *exclusively* as a rule of life to define customs and behaviour, still more if they are used as a bastion against the enemy, they are almost bound to come into conflict with other rules of life – a conflict which will ultimately be self-destructive and, therefore, a particularly dangerous example of the narrow understanding of the *spiritual* with which I began.

Sacred scriptures are not just highly prized pieces of literature, like a Shakespeare play or a Jane Austen novel, which somehow encapsulate a universally recognized human truth. But neither are they collections of 'proof texts' which can be treated as infallible guides catering for *every* human eventuality. Naturally they are filled with much wisdom for human living, but they will always need to be interpreted by the exigencies of the present. The danger – present much more in the prophetic than in the mystical religions – is that a spirituality based on the sacred word can become self-sufficient and exclusivist. Like the ritualism which I criticized in the last chapter, it needs to be corrected by other forms of religious practice. Obedience to the divinely revealed word is not the only way in which God can be known.

CHAPTER 5
Meditation and Prayer

For just as taking a walk, journeying on foot, and running are bodily exercises, so we call Spiritual Exercises every way of preparing and disposing the soul to rid itself of all inordinate attachments, and, after their removal, of seeking and finding the will of God in the disposition of our life for the salvation of our soul.[1]

(St Ignatius of Loyola)

The turn from the materialist West to the supposedly spiritual East, in search of the experience which Christianity has failed to give, has brought with it decidedly mixed results. We have seen gurus fêted from Pune to San Francisco, methods of meditation packaged and sold like any other product of the consumer culture. The worst excesses of that particular phase seem mercifully to have passed; the power of self-obsessed holy men has all too often proved a poor substitute for the dead weight of church structures. A more informed dialogue has taken its place – one which tries to appreciate history and culture, the context in which a religion lives, rather than treats another faith as a quarry which can be ruthlessly exploited to repair the battered edifice of Western culture.

Christians trying to understand their own tradition and people of no religion seeking a faith which sustains and speaks to them are united in the respect they feel for the spiritualities of Hinduism and Buddhism. The immediate enthusiasm for all things Indian may have given way to a more judicious appreciation of truth wherever it is to be found; the fact remains that more and more people – including many Christians – are practising Eastern forms of meditation and deriving enormous benefit from them. Even so, questions remain, particularly about the appropriateness of using Eastern techniques for Christian prayer.

Obedience to the ancient tradition does not preclude their use; rather, if what I have said earlier about the dangers inherent in ritual exclusivism and scriptural fundamentalism is anything like correct, *jñana-yoga* is the necessary complement to *karma-yoga*. For a good many years scores of Buddhist monks have spent periods in Catholic monasteries and Catholic monks and nuns have received similar hospitality and training in Buddhist monasteries of the East. It would be tedious to make a list of all the priests, religious and lay folk in India and the Far East – and in Britain too – for whom Yoga, Zen and T'ai Chi have become as natural a part of their lives as sitting and breathing. Bede Griffiths, William Johnston and Thomas Merton are only the most familiar names. The answer to the question whether Christians can use Eastern techniques of meditation is that Christians *do* use Eastern techniques. A Christian practises Zen and Yoga as a Christian; such forms of meditation do not replace Christian faith with Buddhist or Hindu faith but challenge the meditator to a more radical *Christian* faith.

Someone once asked Merton, cynically, whether he left Jesus outside the Zen meditation hall along with his shoes – a gratuitously insulting remark which shows a profound ignorance of Zen. It is impossible for a Christian to 'leave Jesus outside'. Religious faith cannot be compared to a pair of shoes which can be discarded at will. Even so, it is only right to draw attention to the dangers and risks. Not all Eastern forms of meditation can be integrated into Christian prayer. There are bound to be religious aims and metaphysics which are at variance with Christianity; many parallels and resemblances are too superficial to be reliable guides. Secondly, not all altered or heightened states of consciousness are religious. What, for instance, are we to make of drug-induced experiences? Clearly there are many complex issues to be investigated here. They range from the practical – *What* method? – to the more theological – *Why* method? What do we need techniques of prayer for? More importantly: What is the place of *jñana-yoga*, the way of knowledge, in the Christian life and what is its relationship to what I have called simply the 'Mystery of Christ'?

Christian Prayer: The Prayer of Christ

Let us take this last question first. To write a treatise on Christian prayer is not my intention; it would be neither appropriate nor helpful. Prayer is an expression of faith and the faith of any religious community has a particular character, a character which must be maintained if the integrity of the community is not to be compromised. In discussing Christian prayer, the obvious place to begin is with Jesus' own prayer. Christians are to pray as Jesus prayed – addressing God as Father, recognizing the close and intimate relationship into which they are being drawn. In the Sermon on the Mount Jesus instructs his disciples how to pray by warning them not to 'heap up empty phrases' but to retire into an 'inner room' where their innermost thoughts can be known. They are not to be like the 'hypocrites', people putting on an act before God. Jesus' followers are to present themselves before God *as they are*, not as they think they are or would like people to see them, but with honesty and sincerity. Self-knowledge and a proper appreciation of one's own worth are, therefore, both essential prerequisites for prayer.

Jesus teaches his disciples his special prayer – the Lord's Prayer, which expresses his own relationship with his Father. In establishing this relationship it is God who takes the initiative – just as Jesus emphasizes that 'You did not choose me, but I chose you' (John 15.16). Christian prayer must, therefore, have something of the character of a response. We recognize our own value and worth in so far as we respond to God's loving initiative revealed in Christ. Thus whatever value there may be in technique or methods of prayer, it must be subordinated to the fundamental conviction that God has given or revealed himself to us. Is it not a mistake, therefore, to see prayer as something which we have to *do* in order to put ourselves in touch with God? A Christian approach to prayer begins somewhere else, with the insight that we can do nothing of ourselves, that we need God to do something in us. Thus Paul writes to the Romans that 'we do not know how to pray as we ought, but the Spirit himself intercedes for us with sighs too deep for words' (Rom. 8.26). Throughout that epistle Paul is making an anguished cry for help; he knows his own sinfulness and distance from God, yet coupled with this knowledge is his profound experience of the love of God, that God has come close to him through no merit on his part. Prayer is for Paul the action of the Holy Spirit who 'prays in us' the prayer of Jesus to his Father. What in that case do we do – or not do – to let the Spirit pray in us?

In what follows I want to make two points: that preparation for prayer is an essential part of the proper response to God's initiative and that a spirituality of knowledge, *jñana-yoga*, as it would be called in Indian religion, is not at variance with, but actually supports, the spirituality of ritual with which the earlier part of this book has been concerned. In saying this I am not recommending a spirituality of *gnosis* – one which bases itself on the acquisition of special insight or esoteric knowledge. By knowledge in this case I mean no more than the inner conviction which comes through personal meditation and contemplative prayer. Such a knowledge reinforces faith – that search for meaning which convinces people of the truth of what is celebrated in the liturgy.

Preparation for Prayer

This question of the relationship between liturgical and meditative prayer should not delay us for long. To pick up the point made above about sin and weakness, all of us have experienced at some time what Paul writes about with such power: a sense of sin and distance from God. What is our response? In times of great trial and darkness we tend naturally to pray the harder, more earnestly. Jesus' own prayer in the Garden of Gethsemane may well sustain us; the constant repetition of the phrase from the Lord's Prayer, 'Thy will be done', may be as much as we can manage. Sin, however, has a nasty habit of making its presence felt in more insidious ways. Given a really solid dose of sin (the experience, for example, of betraying a friend, or – perhaps more difficult to accept – the experience of *being* betrayed), prayer can become remarkably easy, a heartfelt plea for forgiveness or support. I suspect, however, that most of us feel distant from God in the daily pressures and distractions of everyday life when the very remembrance of God, let alone particular prayers, becomes incredibly difficult. At such times we may not be asking 'How to carry on?' but 'How to begin?'

One answer is to return to the liturgy, to the more-or-less formal repetition of familiar readings and prayers in company with other people struggling to express their faith. The support of a community can be enormously beneficial; hence the success of charismatic and group prayer. This is only to repeat what I have spoken of earlier: the routine of community celebration which reinforces the symbols of faith sets up what might be called a supportive rhythm of prayer. Anyone beginning to pray, and anyone suffering from the demoralizing distractions of the everyday, needs such a background. Having said that, however, we need to remember that liturgical prayer is not a substitute for the personal prayer of the 'inner room'. The various forms of common prayer – reciting the office, Bible readings, prayer groups, even the Eucharist itself – can encourage mere dependence on the group, whereas they should be leading us to develop a more intimate awareness of God at the heart of our lives. To pray with others may leave us with the sense of having done something and therefore feeling a little better for our efforts; the danger is that prayer can become too much bound up with 'action' – a process of repeating formulae which, we assume, automatically bring us closer to God and God closer to us. Liturgical prayer is where the spiritual life begins for most people, but it cannot remain there. The great truths of the tradition have to be understood and interiorized. The story of Christ, his life, death and resurrection, becomes the Christian's story: the recognition that God comes to us out of love, not because we may have said lots of prayers and attended lots of church services.

Liturgical prayer in common gives way to meditative personal prayer. But if the former can be characterized by a sense of activity, what needs to be *done*, so can the latter. At least part of the suspicion about the use of Eastern methods of meditation in Christian prayer springs from the fear of Pelagianism, the heresy which thought that people could achieve salvation through their own powers. The Christian conviction is that God reaches to us; we cannot by ourselves do anything to 'earn' what is pure gift. I have already made the point that prayer is a response to God's initiative. Certainly this is an insight which it would be disastrous to ignore. But it does not follow that all forms of prayer – liturgical or meditative – must be based on an attitude of passivity. It may be true that God has come close to us in Christ through grace – a pure gift, with no merit on our part. At the same time, there is more to prayer than a passive waiting around for the Spirit to act. In the liturgy there is much that needs to be done in order to pray: preparation is taken for granted. Our concern must be to make sure that the activity of prayer does not become an end in itself. Similarly with meditative prayer, the spirituality of knowledge, there is work to be done. The antidote to Pelagianism cannot be Quietism.

Methods of Prayer

This takes us on to the question of the value of methods of prayer. At the beginning of this chapter I used the somewhat dismissive image of the quarry to caricature one approach to the inter-faith dialogue. Another, more nuanced, approach does not so much seek to find something new which can be incorporated into the existing Christian tradition as allow the dialogue itself to point the way to the insights, truths and practices which are already present. There are plenty of types and methods of prayer, both in the Christian tradition and in other faiths, notably in the many forms of *yoga* which are to be found in Hinduism and Buddhism. Knowledge of the latter should reinforce our appreciation of the former. Christians have a rich tradition of methods of prayer. The opening note of the *Spiritual Exercises* of St Ignatius, for example, begins in good classical fashion by defining its terms: spiritual exercises are analogous with bodily exercises. Ignatius' little handbook is as much concerned for proper physical preparation for prayer as for mental and spiritual development. Yet at no time are the various exercises which 'dispose' a person who prays seen as a Pelagian grasping after 'experience'. The aim is to develop an indifference which leaves God free to act in whatever way *God* may choose. To see prayer as a human activity, a way of disposing or opening ourselves to the transforming action of God's Spirit, need not contradict the fundamental conviction of Christianity that a relationship with God cannot be induced or forced. The teaching of the Indian mystical tradition, as much as Christianity, is that activity must be matched by a certain passivity. Our 'work' is the work of preparation to receive the gift.

That said, we need to understand the context within which the meditative traditions of the East have arisen. Earlier I spoke of karma-yoga, the spirituality which is based in the ritual, in the traditional actions which surround the most significant formal gatherings of the religious community. *Yoga* in this context means simply path, way or practice – an Eastern equivalent of the Ignatian 'spiritual exercise'. In this sense it is just part of what we might call the basic structure underlying all Indian religions, without which neither Hinduism nor Buddhism can properly be understood.

There is no easy answer to the question of origins. They remain shrouded in mystery. We find few traces of *Yoga* in the Veda, which represents the religion of the *brahmin*-priests. Most authorities would agree that *yoga* comes from a different strand in the great complex of Indian religion – that associated with the *sannyasi* or wandering holy man. A superficial view of the practitioner of *yoga* or *yogi* makes him appear as a drop-out, a beggar who exists on the fringes of society. Yet very few conform to the Western caricature – the wild-eyed, long-haired loner who contorts his body into all sorts of odd positions in order to give himself strange otherworldly experiences. In reality he is the one committed to the radical search for personal liberation or *moksha*. As such he is deeply respected by ordinary people who make of him almost a sacrament of the divine. The meaning of *moksha* varies according to one's view of the final end or purpose of humankind. For theistic faiths final salvation is seen as union with God; for the non-theistic, such as Buddhism, it is an impersonal state such as *nirvana*. All religions have some concept approximating to the Indian *moksha*; the individual or the social group seeks for a state of freedom in which the sufferings of the world are no more and a state of eternal bliss or happiness takes their place. Where they differ – and sometimes differ quite radically – is in the basic conception of what people are to be saved from and what they are to be emancipated to.

Religions also differ in the relative weight which is given to what I have described in terms of 'activity' or 'passivity' in prayer. Thus Christianity, anchored in the ancient Hebrew tradition of an utterly holy, transcendent God who has acted in the past to save his people, looks to the same God to fulfil his promises and to become again the source of salvation. Prayer is an expression of hope in God: an attitude to be found at the heart of many of the Psalms. Early Indian religion, on the other hand, is far more agnostic about the power of the gods to save. In one of the most celebrated of the Vedic hymns, for example, the sage asks about the origins of creation: 'What was it that stirred in the beginning?' Question is piled upon question: 'Who really knows? Who will here proclaim it? Whence was it produced? Whence is this creation?' The sage is eventually forced to admit: 'Whence this creation has arisen – perhaps it formed itself or perhaps it did not – the one who looks down on it in the highest heaven, only he knows – or perhaps he does not know' (*Rig Veda* 10.129). The desire to *know* – to be convinced – is one of the most striking features of Indian religion.

To some extent the mood of hesitant speculation which characterizes the hymn illustrates perfectly the failure of ritual religion

63

to engage people at a personal level. In the history of Hinduism we find that in the later Vedic period (800 BCE) a different sort of spirituality begins to make itself felt – that dominated by the individual searcher after truth. The key factors behind what is often called the 'renouncer movement' are still unclear. There was some sort of social upheaval which saw the establishment of urban economies and the consequent displacement of a village-based population. Perhaps consequent upon this, the power of the ritual to command people's allegiance had disappeared, lost in the complex and frankly magical ritualism which had become the preserve of a privileged élite, the *brahmin* caste. Acts of worship which demanded vast expense, many days of preparation, a large number of specialist performers and a passive audience did not do much to answer the religious needs of ordinary folk. Psychologically and religiously the traditional forms of the brahmanical sacrifice were quite inadequate to the task of coping with the popular malaise. The renouncer, *sannyasi*, is also a *yogi*, one who practises meditation. Through his *yoga*-practice he hopes to develop the knowledge or conviction of salvation.

The Practice of Yoga: Harmony and Integration

These rather general remarks may help to set the context in which we can understand the original *religious* meaning of *Yoga*. It should not be defined in terms of a particular aim or even as a 'system of meditation', but simply as *method*, teaching a way to concentrate the attention and, thereby, to gain the assurance of salvation. *Yoga* is a Sanskrit word closely related to the Latin *iugum* which gives us the English 'yoke'. The basic image which explains the aim of the early *sannyasis* is that of the yoking together of beasts in order to get them under control. The *yogi* aims to harness the energy of the senses by subjecting them to the yoke of the mind. Thus *yoga* refers to forms of spiritual exercise which help to concentrate the attention – essential if one is to know *anything*, let alone divine truth. Later many practices typical of the *yoga* tradition were gathered together into a 'classical' system of thought and practice which is described in the famous Yoga-sutras of Patañjali which date from the second to the fifth centuries CE. Later still we find various schools of *yoga* growing up: *Mantra-yoga*, for example, the *yoga* of incantation, or *Hatha-yoga*, literally the '*yoga* of force' but referring to a type of practice which emphasizes liberation achieved through physical as well as spiritual self-control. To repeat: the word refers to *method* or *way*, not to any particular vision or understanding of the *end* of the way. Religiously it is value-free.

What are the key ideas which hold all *yoga*-practice together? The opening verse of the classical Yoga-sutras describes the aim of *yoga* as 'the destruction of the modifications of the mind'. The mind is prone to distraction, forever flitting from one focus of attention to another. How does one learn to stay with just the one subject? *Yoga*, spiritual exercise, is a way by which the mind is anchored and taught to avoid the distractions which dissipate the powers of concentration. According to the texts the aim is to achieve *ekagrata*, literally 'one-pointedness', of concentration – a state of relaxation in which the meditator is aware of one thing only at the centre of consciousness and nothing else. Other typically yogic practices, such as *asana*, posture, which in *hatha-yoga* becomes a regular science of psycho-physical culture, and *pranayama*, breath-control, are basically means to this end. So much all yogic methods have in common: anchoring the attention on a single item of experience.

How do they differ? Clearly the nature of the focus is bound to have an effect on the state of 'none-pointedness'. If the focus is pleasant then the subsequent state of consciousness is bound to be relaxed; if unpleasant then it will produce a feeling of revulsion. Thus the Buddhist practice of meditating on the decaying body is meant to counter evil desires, such as lust, and build up a sense of the transience of all things. On the other hand, meditation on a topic like loving-kindness or on the qualities of the Buddha builds up a sense of compassion for all creatures. The choice of topic depends on the needs of the individual. In both, however, the technique is much the same: to allow the mind to become absorbed in or formed by the stimulus. A Buddhist practice, for instance, is to focus attention on a coloured disc. Gradually the meditator learns to abstract a secondary image from the visual stimulus, one which totally fills the mind. Gradually the meditator trains him or herself to experience more and more rarified levels of consciousness, leading eventually to a state in which there is no longer consciousness of any 'object' or focus of attention. All that remains is a uniformity of consciousness, a state of harmony and peace, in which the distinction between the experiencing 'subject' and the external or separate 'object' has been overcome. A sense of interior integration has been achieved or – as a Hindu meditator might put it – a vision of *dharma*, the order behind creation, is experienced in the heart.

Yoga-practice is all about experiencing harmony and integration. According to one Indian theory of creation the universe comes to be through a disequilibrium in the original first principle. Salvation or *moksha* is thus a matter of restoring the balance. Just as a lack of balance in the three *gunas*, literally 'strands' or 'qualities' – *sattva*, lightness, *rajas*, passion, and *tamas*, darkness – causes the One to become Many, so will their reintegration in the human person return what is Many into what is truly One. Through forms of yogic meditation the restoration of a personal equilibrium is sought. The purpose of *yoga* is to produce the right psychological conditions that one may know oneself and, through knowing self, know the God who is at the heart of each person's 'inner room'.

The Way of Knowledge

Such remarks may go some way towards explaining the central significance of the spirituality of knowledge in Indian religion. A whole culture has been developed to help people see the God who is 'hard to see'. *Jñana-yoga* is the way of those mystics whose aim is to develop an intuition or insight into the nature of the relationship between human and divine. In Hinduism it is found most clearly in the philosophical texts called Upanishads, a whole collection or genre of religious literature the oldest of which goes back to about 700 BCE. The word seems to mean something like 'sitting down near' and refers to the relationship between *guru* and pupil of which the written texts are a record. Anyone reading the Upanishads as a classical summary of the undoubted riches of Indian philosophy or as a practical guide to mystical and meditative techniques is likely to be severely disappointed. The mass of rambling speculation, obscure dialogue and gnomic utterances which makes up the twelve or thirteen classical texts does not reduce itself to any sort of consistency. What does emerge with great clarity, however, is the Indian fascination with the spiritual dimension of the world, not with the Absolute as somehow beyond or separate from the world but as bound up with the world of appearances. A friend who wrote to me from India recently said that he found that

Hindus had a highly developed sense of the spiritual but little sense of the transcendent. He was half-right. The point is that the Transcendent is not separate from the world but is immediate and already present to anyone who truly wants to see. The Upanishads are as practical and as religious as the hymns of the Vedas. The question asked, however, is no longer the Vedic 'What is the cause of this creation?' but rather the more severely practical 'How is one to know?'

To seek in the Upanishads for a single coherent doctrine of the Ultimate is about as realistic as asking for a summary of Christian belief in a couple of sentences. The texts do not lend themselves to simple synthesis. What we find are two sets of questions: first, about the nature of that One originating principle from which the whole of the created universe has emanated forth, and, secondly, about the nature of that single unchanging principle which gives the human person coherence and continuity. The two terms which are used interchangeably in a sometimes confusing fashion are *brahman*, 'Holy Power', the originating power of the universe, and *atman*, the Soul, Self or innermost ground of all that exists. This is the heart of the wisdom of the Upanishads, what at first sight seems to be a simple equivalence: *brahman* is one with *atman*. The precise meaning of this extraordinarily daring idea has occupied Indian philosophers ever since. The Upanishads ponder over many an abstract philosophical issue; more importantly, however, they aim to be practical, leading the initiate into the 'cave of the heart' – there, where one is most truly self or *atman*, to know the Ultimate, *brahman*. What is being spoken of is a state of unified consciousness, in which there is no sense of subject and object, a pure *self*-consciousness which is the consciousness of *brahman*:

> If a person knew the atman with the thought 'I am he!' with what desire, for love of what would he cling to the body? He who has found and awakened to the atman ... he is the maker of everything, for he is the creator of all; the world is his; indeed, he is the world itself. (Brihadaranyaka Upanishad 4.4.12)

Ritual and Meditation

There are many ways in which this type of spirituality is very different from the ritualism of which we have already spoken at some length. But there is an important similarity. In the Upanishads we find an intriguing, yet totally enigmatic, fascination with changing states of consciousness, particularly dream states and states achieved in meditation which appear to transcend the dreamless state, leading to an experience considered close to a merging into the Ultimate *brahman* from which all originated. How to distinguish between such 'altered states' is a highly complex question which will occupy us in the next chapter. All I want to note at this stage is that the motif of pilgrimage is to be found in both the spirituality of ritual and that of meditation. There is a parallel between the external, literal pilgrimage of *karma-yoga* and the internal liturgy of *jñana-yoga*, in which the individual makes a 'pilgrimage' of self-discovery, a journey within. Just as the ritual is concerned with rehearsing the great truths which keep the universe in being, so the meditation of the *yogi* performs an interior ritual – but one which spiritually and psychologically is more effective.

In noting this similarity between liturgical and meditative prayer it is important to emphasize that, however different the forms of prayer which they contain, they are united by a single aim: the entry into what the Upanishads call the 'cave of the heart' or what Jesus calls the 'inner room', there to be with 'the Father who sees in secret'. Various methods of prayer are used in the East to help people to relax and to enter into a mood of stillness and receptivity. If what I have said above is correct, then there is no reason in theory why they should not be used by Christians to help them to pray. To repeat: *yoga* is method not aim. In practice a judicious choice needs to be exercised, preferably under direction; not all *yoga* methods can be assimilated to the Christian's aim of responding to the invitation of the Father. A certain unity of purpose in all methods of prayer – Christian and Indian – can, however, be found.

In speaking of the liturgy I pointed out that the relationship of faith is evoked by key symbols, prayers or phrases. Similarly in meditation: to centre the mind on a familiar word or phrase can lead to the heart of the relationship with God. Jesus' use of the single word 'Abba' is the obvious example. All the meditator does is centre the mind – literally 'con-centrating' it – on a focus of attention which is *already* the heart of his or her life. In Indian religions such a meaningful word or phrase is called a *mantra*, literally an 'instrument of thought', a word which has the power to evoke in the heart the sense of Sacred Mystery. Such a concept is not foreign to Christianity. Christian versions are to be found in such authoritative spiritual writers as John Cassian, St Ignatius of Loyola and the author of *The Cloud of Unknowing*. Words like '*Abba*', 'Lord', '*Kyrie Eleison*', '*Maranatha*', or forms of the Jesus Prayer, can be the point of entry into the cave of the heart where one is 'at home', truly oneself, and God can be allowed to be God.

Note

1   *The Spiritual Exercises of St Ignatius of Loyola*, trans. Louis J. Puhl SJ (Chicago: Loyola University Press, 1951), para. 1.

CHAPTER 6

Discerning Divine Mystery

Before you study Zen, mountains are mountains and rivers are rivers. While you study Zen, mountains are no longer mountains and rivers are no longer rivers. When you have attained enlightenment, mountains are again mountains and rivers are again rivers.

(Ch'ing Yuan)

The most moving religious service I ever attended took place in most unpromising circumstances: at midnight, sitting in the dust, surrounded by a congregation of Gujerati villagers of whose language I could understand not a word. It would take too long to describe the incredible story which brought me there. I was with a priest friend and we were celebrating the anniversary of the death of some villagers – two Hindus and two Christians – killed in a nasty piece of communal violence the year before. After an evening spent drinking seemingly endless saucers of tea in one house after another we eventually joined the people of the village for Mass out on the plain in front of the tombs of the dead men. It was a particularly poignant and moving occasion, deeply prayerful and laden with emotion. At the end of the Mass the head catechist sang a lament for his dead son. I can still hear the sound of his voice echoing in the stillness of the night. And I did not need to know any Gujerati to understand what he had sung.

No doubt we can all recount exact memories of our profoundest religious experiences: the times when we were deeply moved or in some way felt and understood the closeness of God. Nor can there be any doubt that the sort of experience I have described enhances religious consciousness to a remarkable degree. And yet the role of experience in religion is complex. The object of experience, as I have insisted, cannot be God but only God's effects, the 'signs' of God's presence and creative power. What justifies our speaking of such signs as 'inspired' by or immediately dependent on God? Dreams and altered states of consciousness are often interpreted as profoundly meaningful. And so they may be – in certain circumstances. But what are we to make of states induced by drugs or physiological stress? It is too easy to speak of religious experience in terms of 'self-validating' revelations, voices and visions, for who is to know that the voice of comfort is not, in fact, the voice of delusion?

Earlier I spoke about faith as the search for meaning: people infer from the order or beauty of creation or from some aspect of their experience which is inherently meaningful the existence of what I have called Ultimate Value. Through ritual and the traditions vested in the sacred texts the religious community evokes and sustains such experiences. These experiences may justifiably be called religious, for they are the experiences of religious people – people of faith. At some point, however, we have to make a distinction between faith and credulity. The former springs from the conviction that the world we experience is not ultimately irrational, that meaning is to be found. The latter arises when fear of the unknown takes over, when the search for the meaning or mystery behind phenomena and events gives way to a morbid fascination with the mysterious itself – precisely because it is mysterious and not meaningful. At this point it is all too easy to point to all sorts of 'mysterious' human experiences as somehow superhuman, that is to say, as 'signs' by which God may be 'known'.

The Nature of Experience

The first task is to come to terms with that much-abused term 'experience'. An experience, whether of world-shattering proportions, such as Paul being blinded on the road to Damascus or the Buddha's enlightenment, or something more common, such as my being moved by a Mozart string quartet, or you reading the words on this page, implies a change of consciousness. Obviously there are different forms of experience and many different ways in which experience is mediated or identified; various factors may affect the way we feel about or react to the world around us – temperament, the time of day, the weather, the news, the latest disaster to befall our favourite football club. Experiences tend to be classified according to their context. Emotional or intellectual experiences are the most common – the sense of being moved or understanding something – but there are also aesthetic experiences and moral experiences. Our state of consciousness is changed by circumstances around us. The fact that it is sometimes very difficult to draw an exact line between various types of experience only underlines the very human tendency to categorize – and therefore to control and limit – experience.

What, then, is the difference between religious experience and, say, aesthetic experience? We can speak of religious experience as a feeling or state of mind caused by factors sometimes held to be beyond explanation but more often than not resulting from a particular religious concern or commitment. One would expect to have a religious experience in a church or listening to Billy Graham but not watching *Match of the Day* or a Party Political Broadcast. That there are special or privileged moments which can be labelled specifically 'religious' or 'mystical' is clear, but, as I have noted before, few people have 'Damascus road experiences' or base their faith-commitment on a clearly definable feeling or sense. When we ordinarily talk of religious experience we are referring not to a particular *type* of experience but to the way the *whole of life* is experienced. It is simply not the case that all religious experiences are extraordinary or fit neatly into a category called 'religious' which differentiates them from – say – moral or aesthetic experience. Nor does religious commitment or belief in God depend on my having had a particular type of religious experience. Rather, if what I have said about faith is correct, then we should consider as 'religious experience' any experience which is interpreted as such; that is to say interpreted as having a religious character or meaning in virtue of which it manifests to us something which we consider to be of ultimate power or value. Thus, for example, I may experience a healing or escape from injury as a miracle. Similarly the people of Israel saw the 'hand of Yahweh' in their deliverance from Egypt; the Aryans of the Vedic times in India experienced the closeness of the Divine in natural events such as the great monsoon and interpreted them as the acts of various *devas* or gods. A number of events or processes may be *experienced as* religious.

Obviously there are a number of problems here – mainly about interpretation, about what counts and what does not count as religious. Leaving that to one side for the moment, let us pick up the problem with which the last chapter was concerned: the nature of a particular type of religious experience, what we might call the extraordinary or mystical, which results from deep meditation. Does what I have said above invalidate such experience?

Experiencing the Extraordinary

What makes such experiences extraordinary is that the mystic claims to have had some sort of a *direct* experience of the transcendent; experience is mediated in some special way not open to everyone. Consciousness is changed so that ordinary categories of description seem not to apply; very often the mystic even speaks as if the ordinary ways of experiencing and knowing are being by-passed. Clearly we must accept the possibility – even probability – that certain privileged persons can have experiences which are to be ascribed to the direct intervention of divine power. This does not mean, however, *either* that all such claims are validly ascribed *or* that the presence of the divine *must* be experienced in this particular way. If God is God, then there can be no limits to the modes of divine presence to humankind.

The obvious distinction to be made is between the preternatural and the supernatural. That *yogis* can arrest their breathing and perform acts of incredible physical endurance, that mystics can report extraordinary inner visions and people of great psychic energy can extend their range of vision and hearing are matters of report which are by no means to be dismissed as sheer make-believe. No doubt there are plenty of charlatans about; when the teachers of Transcendental Meditation who began by teaching a simple and highly effective method of breathing in harmony with a personal *mantra*, start promising levitation one may be justified in drawing a line. At this point spirituality slides inexorably into the wilder fantasies of science fiction. But it is clearly impossible to dismiss all claims to special experiences as sheer make-believe. The record of mystical experience within a supposedly 'non-mystical' religion like Christianity is long and well-documented. What are we to make of St Teresa of Avila and St John of the Cross, for example?

To say that such-and-such an individual has had a particular experience means no more than that. Claims to mystical experience do not – and cannot – tell us anything which is *necessarily* true about the supernatural, which is no more to be controlled by method than God is an object of experience. What we experience we may well interpret as the effects of God's activity in the world. Whether we are correct to do this is another matter.

Each religion has its own wealth of wisdom in interpreting religious experience – what in Christian spirituality is often called the 'discernment of spirits'. There are some obvious criteria: a sense of peace and harmony, a strengthening of faith and a growing capacity to overcome anxiety and doubt. The problem is that human beings – even those motivated by what they take to be the best of intentions – have an enormous capacity for self-deception. Where are we to look for guidance?

Perhaps the first point to note is that the concept of spiritual direction is not a peculiarly Christian preserve. In fact Eastern traditions of yogic meditation are far more insistent than Christianity on the central role of the teacher or guide. Meditation or spiritual exercise is not something to be learned from a book, but directly from someone who is already steeped in the tradition and has the necessary skill and discernment to choose the right methods for particular individuals. Anyone reading Hindu or Buddhist scriptures for the secret of 'how it is done' is liable to be disappointed. Technique – preparation, posture, forms of relaxation – has its place but is subordinate to the relationship of trust established with a qualified teacher. Such a *jñanin*, a 'knowledgeable one' who really has experienced the secret of the Divine which the ritual only obscures, embodies the wisdom of the tradition and ensures that correct guidance is given and that the major pitfalls are avoided.

There is, however, an even more important criterion of discernment to be noted. I began by insisting that spirituality must avoid a dichotomy of 'this world' and 'the next world'. To speak of the religious is to speak of what is most profoundly human – not the esoteric and extraordinary but that which opens us to the possibility of knowing the transcendent in the ordinary and everyday. And if what I have said about religious experience above is correct, then it follows that we must avoid a concentration on the 'special' phenomena of mysticism at the expense of the context within which – and *only* within which – they can be interpreted. The Buddha, for example, perhaps the greatest spiritual director of all, tried to warn his disciples not to be seduced by preternatural 'powers' which were an inevitable but not necessarily significant accompaniment to the spiritual journey. Mystical experiences are not to be confused with the one object of meditation, true enlightenment, *nirvana*. In what follows I want to show that this typically Buddhist attitude to experience can be of immense benefit in helping us to identify the truly significant moments in our lives.

The Buddha's Spiritual Path

The great upheaval in Indian religion which resulted in a reaction against the formalism of Vedic sacrificial religion parallels in some ways the search for religious meaning that is typical of our own day. Siddhartha, the dissatisfied prince who became the Buddha, is only the most famous figure from that era; others, notably Mahavira the Jina, the 'victor', the founder of Jainism, are not to be forgotten. Almost despite themselves, for neither Buddha nor Jina was interested in any personal position or prestige, they attracted followers to their unambiguous teaching and stark ascetical practice.

It would, however, be quite wrong to lump all ascetics – especially Indian ones – unceremoniously together as if they all teach the same thing. Siddhartha Gautama joined the 'renouncer movement' in Indian religion but was quite unambiguous *both* in his rejection of the ritual tradition dominated by the brahmins *and* in his criticism of the excesses of the yogic practice of his day. The Buddha actually left his first teachers because he found that, while they taught a *jñana-yoga*, or way of knowledge, it was not based on the pursuit of *nirvana* but merely on the achieving of various levels of consciousness.

This latter point needs to be examined carefully. Buddhism arose from the Hindu milieu which we have already looked at briefly. It was born of a reaction against that type of spirituality which had developed into a highly complex semi-magical ritual. This stressed the importance of knowledge, but the sort of knowledge involved – concerned with arcane interpretations, an extremely mysterious pseudo-science – remained always a sort of vested interest of the few initiated priests. The ordinary people hardly got a look-in. Which is why a different type of ritual developed for the lower castes – the sort of thing briefly described earlier in the dance-drama. But the young Siddhartha Gautama, the *bodhisattva* or Buddha-to-be, also rejected much of the ascetical teaching which was being proposed as a sort of substitute for the experience the ritual failed to give. Partly this was because he saw in it no more than a meaningless self-torture, partly because he could see that it inhibited the very thing it was designed to achieve: a vision of what is ultimately true.

To simplify somewhat, we can say that Buddhism was another attempt to develop a form of religion which would appeal to ordinary people and recognize the religious value of ordinary experience. True – the Buddha was hardly an ordinary person; he was not a *brahmin* but he does seem to have come from a high caste. The social background of Buddhism is all too easily ignored, but it should remind us of one important fact. All the schools and sects which developed from the original enlightenment experience – some highly mystical and philosophical, others devotional and given to ritual and an abundance of fanciful myth – all of them have this much in common: they are an expression of the Buddha's desire to teach Truth or *dharma* to all people, all 'sentient beings'. Knowledge of the Truth does not involve an esoteric *gnosis* or a certain special type of experience but the acceptance of the ordinary, *whatever is given in the present*.

Coming to Terms with Life

What did the Buddha teach? We first have to see the problem of human existence as the Buddha saw it. Only if we diagnose the situation correctly, said the Buddha, are we likely to realize a solution. In the untranslatable Pali word the problem is *dukkha*. To call it 'suffering' misses the richness of the term; it refers to all that is unsatisfactory and unpleasant, whatever brings actual pain, physical or mental, and whatever frustrates our human need for meaning and purpose. The Buddha saw himself essentially as a practical guide to the Middle Way, a physician who prescribes treatment for anyone who seriously wants a cure. The Four Noble Truths which he elaborated are best understood by analogy with medical terminology. The bald statement that life is *dukkha*, the First Noble Truth, is the diagnosis; what the Buddha teaches is the cure, not a way of avoiding *dukkha*, still less some sort of substitute, but a way of confronting it and by dealing with the root causes overcoming its effects. The cure is the unconditioned *nirvana*, the Third Noble Truth; and the way to achieve that cure, the Buddha's own remedy, is the Fourth Noble Truth, the Noble Eightfold Path, a series of eight factors which together go to make up a lifetime of careful ethical, ascetical and meditative practice: Right View, Right Thought, Right Speech, Right Action, Right Livelihood, Right Effort, Right Mindfulness, Right Concentration.

The Second Noble Truth, the cause of *dukkha*, is even more difficult to understand correctly than the First. Simply to refer to the famous triad, greed, hatred and delusion – shown in many a

Buddhist illustration of the wheel of life as a cock, a rat and a snake all swallowing each other's tails – does not get us all that far. Desire, grasping and ignorance are all part of what it means to be human and are not to be overcome by sheer asceticism. In a subtle way the desire to understand, to find meaning, to seek purpose and fulfilment – still more the desire for experiences – is self-defeating; it brings about *dukkha* because what we are doing is searching for the impossible. We expect to find what is permanent and unchanging in a world characterized not by stability but by change. All that experience – *any* experience – gives is, in the Buddhist phrase, 'coming to be and passing away'.

The implications of these key ideas – the knottier problems of Buddhist teaching, such as the conditioned nature of reality and the meaning of *nirvana* – will have to wait for my final chapter. For the moment let us stay with the diagnosis and ask why the Buddhist is so concerned to 'see the problem correctly' and, secondly, how this is to be done.

The first question is relatively easy to answer. We have to come to terms with life *as it is*, not as we would like it to be. In the last chapter we had a brief look at the society of the Buddha's day, which was formed very much by the social and religious malaise of the seventh and sixth centuries BCE. There we noted an earnest searching for religious experience and an enormous amount of argument and speculation about the meaning of existence. Teachers abounded who promised this or that experience as the way to the Ultimate. Before his enlightenment the young Buddha-to-be studied with two of them and rejected their teaching as unsatisfactory. He eventually found his own way and discovered the eternal *dharma*, the truth which he proceeded to preach to five ascetics who had at an earlier stage accompanied him on his search. They too, we are told, were enlightened; such was the beginning of Buddhism.

Compared with other forms of ascetical and contemplative training, this path does not seem to be in any way remarkable or to differ very much from what we might expect to find in any monastically inspired tradition of spirituality. But there is one element in the Noble Eightfold Path which marks it off quite radically from its Indian forebears. This is in many ways that most typically Buddhist of all meditative practices – Right Mindfulness. To understand it correctly let us put it into its proper context.

The Second Noble Truth is given as 'this thirst which produces re-existence and re-becoming, bound up with passionate greed'. The word translated here as thirst means craving or desire, including the more subtle attachment to personal ideas, ideals and beliefs which may inhibit true freedom. As we have already noted, the analyses of the cause of suffering vary considerably, from thirst and ignorance to the triad of greed, hatred and delusion. Much of this can be overcome by what is described in the sixth stage of the Eightfold Path – Right Striving or Effort. This can be understood in purely negative terms as the constant control of evil inclinations and impulses. To use the popular image which occurs in the texts: as the tortoise draws in its limbs on sensing danger, so should the sage try to guard and control his senses. But, as the Buddha says, if we think simply in these terms the deaf and the blind must have controlled their senses. True discipline begins with Right Effort – meaning mental energy and perseverance. This, however, is not an end in itself but a necessary predisposition for the final stages of the Path. Effort has to be *Right* and what prevents Effort simply becoming a one-sided concern for ascetical practice is the next stage on the Noble Eightfold Path. Effort becomes Right by being tempered by mindfulness to produce Right Concentration.

Practising Mindfulness

In comparing the Buddhist teaching on asceticism and Yoga with what is to be found in other forms of yogic practice, it is clear that what is specific to Buddhism is the emphasis on Mindfulness. The Sanskrit word behind it is *smriti* – remembrance or 'calling to mind', not a reminiscence about the past but the bringing of the past into the present, seeing everything in the light of the present moment. In the famous sermon on the fruits of being a recluse the Buddha says:

> A monk applies himself either in going forward or back; in looking straight on or looking away; in bending or stretching; in wearing robes or carrying the bowl; in eating, drinking, chewing or savouring; in attending to the calls of nature; in walking, in standing, in sitting, in falling asleep, in waking; in speaking or in keeping silence; in all these he applies full attention. (*Digha Nikaya* 1.70)

Those last two words – 'full attention' – are crucially important. Whatever you are doing, says the Buddha, simply be conscious of that and nothing else. Throughout the day try to be conscious of everything you do, however ordinary or trivial. Attention must be paid to the present moment and the present action. Whatever is done is to be done *mindfully*: with careful attention to every detail until one is minutely aware of every sensation, every reaction, every thought or feeling. Normally we do not observe what is *actually* happening, only what we *think* is happening. Very rarely do we pay full attention to the present and learn to experience what is given to consciousness without distorting reality by imposing on it our rather ill-considered and sometimes short-sighted categories.

Buddhism is all about seeing correctly, about accepting reality as it actually exists. One of my favourite Zen stories concerns the young monk who returns in an excited state to the monastery to tell his teacher about the marvellous progress he has made on the way to enlightenment. The master is unimpressed. 'When you entered the meditation hall,' he asks, 'how did you leave your sandals? The left upon the right or the right upon the left?' 'I have no idea,' says the monk. 'How can I be expected to notice such things?' 'If you do not notice such things, how can you be enlightened?' comes the reply. Only the one who sees everything clearly and correctly can expect to make progress on the Way.

True mindfulness is not achieved without long hours of practice in which – eventually – the meditator achieves a state of true openness or indifference. The word found in the Pali texts of the Theravada school is *upekkha*, literally 'looking on'. This is a quality of consciousness which comes at the end of a number of stages of meditation called *jhana*. What the texts describe is a process of purification in which various hindrances to enlightenment are purged and a simplified state of consciousness is developed. Taken in its fullness, the Eightfold Path is the equivalent of what is often spoken of in Christian texts as the 'threefold way' of purgative, illuminative and unitive stages. The last stage described by the Buddha is not *nirvana* – for *nirvana* is beyond description – but this attitude of *upekkha*, a state of tranquillity and acceptance which leaves one on the threshold of *nirvana*. The meditator is quite free from all emotional disturbances, both good and bad; there is only an inner clarity of vision and purpose, 'looking on' with equanimity.

In the Buddha's practice of mindfulness is described a sort of qualified asceticism: plenty of emphasis is put on purging and purifying disordered tendencies, but with the overall aim of producing a state of consciousness which is deeply aware of each and every stimulus, every change of consciousness – the world as it really is.

On the Death of Self

To return, then, to the problem with which we began: How do we tell the difference between the voice of comfort and the voice of delusion? Discernment is never easy, but in Buddhism, as in Christianity, the key to progress is death to self. No amount of physical or psychological trickery can grasp *nirvana*. Such is the experience of the Buddha's life. It is significant that the unenlightened Gautama rejected the way pressed upon him by his two yogic teachers. He knew it was possible to transcend the experiences which he was taught, that they were no more the ultimate *nirvana* which he sought than any kind of feeling caused by an expanded consciousness. *Nirvana* is quite other; it is not to be 'achieved' by raising consciousness to a higher level as if the Ultimate is somehow to be caught sitting at the end of a massively long ladder. That is the fundamental mistake: giving some sort of ultimate significance to what is really a this-worldly experience. All too easily we allow our own self-projections to get in the way, making God in our own image, reducing *nirvana* to something preternatural. But, if *nirvana* represents Ultimate Value then no purely human effort will realize it, for there is – literally –'no thing' to be realized.

The contemplative quality of *upekkha*, born of mindfulness, is something from which all people of faith can learn. But is there more to it than a sense of detachment from a world of suffering, impermanence and insubstantiality? It would be easy to interpret the Buddha's teaching in a fatalistic sort of way, except that it is impossible to overlook the reverence the Buddhist feels before the mystery of creation and his deep sense of compassion for the lot of suffering humanity. Only the one who is being truly mindful – 'looking on' without words or images – avoids the danger of reducing that mystery to purely human terms. In Zen, which takes the casting off of images much farther than any form of Christian mysticism, there is the famous saying: 'If you meet the Buddha on the road, kill him.' The human form of the Buddha is at best a useful prop for the beginner and at worst a snare, a projection of the human mind which can subvert true progress. *Nirvana* is pure mystery and must be allowed to remain so.

Buddhist asceticism, part of the great tradition of Yoga, is not a form of self-improvement therapy nor a foolproof method of entering into the mystery of the Eternal. The aim is to acquire a right ordering of human desire through the development of a contemplative freedom and equanimity. There are, of course, many differences between Buddhism and traditional forms of Christian spirituality. The Middle Way has no sense of personal sin or offence against a loving God of creation; there is no radical conversion towards a person to whom one is intimately related; there is no equivalent of the spirituality of loving devotion.

In the end, however, the similarities may turn out to be more significant. There are many parallels to be drawn. The essential outlines of the story of an Ignatius of Loyola, a Francis of Assisi, a Siddhartha Gautama are not that different. The central motivation of their lives is much the same: a deep personal experience of the Absolute Reality and a desire, founded on compassion, to share that sense of Mystery with others. The pattern of life – searching for the Ultimate Truth and leading others on the way – is one that repeats itself in both Christianity and Buddhism. Both demand a radical detachment and loss of self; both stress the development of a contemplative consciousness; both lead to an awareness of the mystery of reality yet both stress that the way to find these is *in* the immediate, the ordinary and the everyday.

Christian spirituality always starts with faith based on the vision of an active God, the righteous yet compassionate Yahweh revealed in the Bible, the Father who makes known his love in a human being. The Christian life is all about coming to terms with the implications of this faith: human beings learning from God-with-us what it means to be human. God is already at work in the world, reconciling all things to himself, and asking that those called in Christ co-operate in the building of the Kingdom. The problem is not to arouse the enthusiasm to follow Christ (that rarely seems to be the problem in a prophetic religion) but to channel that enthusiasm in the right way. Desire, even for the best, can lead well-intentioned folk astray unless they first learn to see the world as God sees it, from the standpoint of eternity. This is where the Buddha starts, not so much finding God in all things, but seeing all things as One, as part of that Ultimate Mystery of which all Indian scriptures in their different ways speak. The Buddha tells his followers to be mindful and aware of whatever is presented to their experience. Enlightenment means recognizing that all things *already* possess the Buddha-nature.

The key to 'discerning the mystery' is to see that it is already there, in everyday experience. Buddhism and Christianity begin from very different directions and with very different premisses but the fundamental dynamic of the two traditions remains the same: action and contemplation, asceticism and mysticism, meet in an attitude of equanimity and openness without which the signs of Divine Mystery may not be discerned.

CHAPTER 7

Love for God and the God of Love

> *'Bear me in mind, love me and worship me, sacrifice, prostrate your-*
> *self to me; so will you come to me, I promise you truly, for you are*
> *dear to me. Give up all things of law, turn to me, your only refuge, for*
> *I will deliver you from all evils; have no care.'*
>
> (Bhagavad Gita 18.65–6)

The first major Hindu temple I ever saw was that dedicated to Śri Minaksi in Madurai, one of the most ancient cities of Tamil Nadu in South India. It came as a bit of a shock. I don't know what I expected to see as I set off through the crowded bazaar – presumably some great sacred fortress set well away from the cacophony of the crowd. Temples, like churches and other sacred sites, are reserved in the popular imagination for prayer and meditation. Whatever their size one somehow expects a stately presence which induces a feeling of peace and relaxation. Photographs of South Indian temples I had seen in plenty – distant, exotic, mysterious piles of sculpture – but nothing had prepared me for the explosion of shapes and colours which suddenly confronted me. The temple was at the heart of the city. In fact the city seemed to grow out of it like a gigantic web, winding alleys and dusty paths all converging on the great square walls which marked the formal boundary of the sacred space. Rounding a corner I found myself staring at a great mountain of creatures stretching up into the sky to end in two enormous horns which glinted in the sunlight. These extraordinary encrustations represented gods and demons, humans and animals, the whole of creation arrayed to welcome pilgrims and to remind them of the purpose of their visit. This mythological riot was matched by the cheerful chaos which surrounded the gateways as pilgrims sought to enter into the presence of the Divine, the object of their long journey almost in sight.

83

My dumbfounded contemplation was eventually interrupted by an old man who said with a smile, 'Wonderful, isn't it? Would you like me to show you round?' Guides in Hindu temples are often long-winded and ignorant, but his one was both succinct and knowledgeable. He led me through the gateway at the base of the mountain, where we left our sandals, and on into the first hall, its ceilings covered in paintings of the elephant-headed god Ganesh. There he proceeded to introduce me to the religious life of the temple and to tell me about things I could never have discovered on my own. Thanks to him I got a first-rate introduction to the temple and a sense of what went on there – and why. He showed me the courtyards and galleries, the bathing tanks and innumerable shrines, the entrances to the two sanctuaries (as a non-Hindu I was not allowed to enter) and the great pillared hall. He explained the history of the temple, the main festivals of the city and the myths associated with the two deities worshipped there: the goddess Minaksi and the god Sundareśvarar, a form of the great god Śiva.

Since then I have become better informed about Hindu myth; despite the attentions of some very inadequate guides I have found my way round even bigger and more splendid temples, been impressed by the grandeur of their architecture and marvelled at the complex theology which the very buildings themselves can be seen to represent. But one aspect of that first experience will always remain in the memory, something which my guide pointed out to me: the deep devotion which contact with the temple precinct produced in the people who thronged the courts and sanctuaries. There seemed to be something sacred and holy about the temple itself.

Devotional spirituality, what Hindus refer to as *bhakti-yoga*, is, at once, the simplest and most diffuse of the three. Less formal and more intimate than the way of ritual, less austere and more human than the way of mystical knowledge, it presents the religious quest in terms of a personal relationship, the intimate knowledge which comes from the giving and response of lovers. At the same time there are myriad manifestations of devotionalism which, often including disparate elements of the other two, are not to be reduced to one archetype or model. It is, perhaps, the most difficult spirituality to understand. Like the Śri Minaksi temple, it seems to encompass the whole of life itself.

Symbols and the Sacramental

I used the theme of pilgrimage to explain the relationship between liturgical and mystical spirituality, explaining the latter as the internalizing of the ritual journey to the centre of the universe, and it makes sense to begin here in trying to come to terms with the way of devotion. That temples, churches and mosques should evoke a sense of the sacred is scarcely surprising. Pilgrimage centres are nothing if not visual reminders of key events or some great truth of the tradition. This is particularly true of the religions of India, but it also applies to the prophetic religions.

The obvious example is Mecca, but I prefer to concentrate on Jerusalem since it is held sacred by all three faiths, Judaism, Christianity and Islam. Jerusalem is not just the city of David and therefore a symbol of Jewish aspirations, celebrated as Zion, the holy mountain on which God has set his king (Ps. 2.6). It is also a sign of the contact between God and humanity, the source of the river of life which will flow out of the temple precinct, bringing God's salvation to all peoples (Ezek. 47.1–12; Zech. 14.8). To enter the temple is to sense the power of God's promise, made originally to Abraham, that he would always remain with his people; it is to become one with all those holy men and women, prophets and messengers of God, who have heard and proclaimed the Word. For Muslims Jerusalem is the beginning of Muhammad's night journey when he is taken up through the heavens into the very presence of God (sura 17). The Dome of the Rock on the site of David's temple marks the spot, and to this day remains a potent symbol of the common ancestry and bitter rivalry of these two semitic faiths.

For Christians too Jerusalem is a vivid reminder of their beginnings in the story of Jesus. A century after the crucifixion of Jesus the city was destroyed by the Romans and for most of its turbulent history it has been ruled by Muslims. The Middle Ages saw a clash of religious empires. Christian crusaders briefly gained control of the holy city. Since then Christians have learned to appreciate its purely spiritual significance. Nevertheless the places associated with Jesus have always had an enormous hold over the imagination. In the New Testament, of course, there are those passages which state categorically that Christ himself replaces both the temple and the holy city. In talking to the woman of Samaria, for instance, Jesus says that 'the hour is coming when neither on this mountain nor in Jerusalem will you worship the Father' (John 4.21), while the obscure theology of the epistle to the Hebrews is a grand meditation on the nature of sacred space: 'For here we have no lasting city, but we seek the city which is to come' (Heb. 13.14). But as long as men and women remain creatures of flesh and blood their religion has got to retain a respect and a role not just for what can be thought but for what can be sensed and touched and felt as well. Sacred places, centres of pilgrimage, are important because the practice of religion is not a matter of taking people away from what is truly human but of reinforcing and building on what Christians refer to as the 'sacramental': those privileged or symbolic moments of everyday life when the sacred is almost tangibly present.

Signs of the Mystery

Symbols are more than signs. Signs point to something quite specific while symbols have the power to unlock the imagination, to put us in touch with our deepest aspirations and experiences – in short, as we have noted earlier, to evoke faith. Our most important memories are preserved by images and pictures. Whether we are speaking of the sculptured cycle of creation blazoned across the *gopurams* of the Śri Minaksi temple or the intricate decoration based on verses from the Qur'an which covers the walls of the Dome of the Rock or even the tawdry statues and incense-soaked stations of the cross which are so much part of Roman Catholic piety, there are many ways – many very *human* ways – in which the sense of the divine is channelled.

Symbols are never restricted in their power. For a Christian, Christ is the symbol or sacrament of God, in whom God can be said to have fulfilled the ancient revelation and to have become truly Emmanuel, 'God-with-us'. In John's Gospel Jesus is the one come down from heaven. The signs which he gives do not portray a wonder-worker, but point the way to God. In Christ all people find blessing (Eph. 1.3ff.); on being lifted up, he will draw them all to himself (John 12.32). The series of great signs in the fourth gospel – from Cana to the resurrection itself – witness to Christ as Christ witnesses to the Father. As the author comments at the end of the gospel, these signs 'are written that you may believe that

Jesus is the Christ, the Son of God, and that believing you may have life in his name' (John 20.31).

If this is so, then nothing is profane: there can be no arbitrary limit put on the signs of God's self-revelation. Does this mean there are no distinctions, between Jew and Greek, between slave and free? Paul certainly thought so, 'for you are all one in Christ Jesus' (Gal. 3.28). Yet it took the early Church some time to realize that 'in Christ' the law was not so much abrogated as fulfilled. The ritual prescriptions of the Jewish law obviously weighed heavily. In the Acts of the Apostles, for instance, Peter sees a great vision of 'something descending, like a great sheet ... In it were all kinds of animals and reptiles and birds of the air.' Peter is hungry and a voice tells him to eat. He refuses, for 'I have never eaten anything that is common or unclean', to which the voice replies: 'What God has cleansed, you must not call common' (Acts 10.9–16). All things may now speak of or point to God. Peter and Paul learned their lesson: that God's blessing is not limited to those who adhere to the ideology defined by the law. Christians, no more than any other people of faith, cannot afford to put any arbitrary limit on the possible signs of God's presence. To learn how to look, to contemplate creation with the eyes of faith, faith needs those privileged means of access which somehow point in the right direction. What is more, it needs an ever-growing sense of where those signs, the symbols which speak of the divine presence, are to be found.

All religions contain such symbols. In the Orthodox Church a rich theology surrounds devotion to the icon which, far from being a nice bit of decoration, is a way of entering into the mystery of Christ, the revelation of God's love. Icons are special signs of that love. And in Hinduism – a religion which is almost obsessed with finding the divine in the human, *brahman* in *atman* – the image of the god has a crucially important role to play in the development and nurturing of devotion. An icon – Krishna playing his flute, Rama in the company of his beloved Sita, Śiva in the form of the *lingam*, the sign of life and creativity – puts the worshipper in touch with a story in which he or she somehow feels involved. Whatever goes on in church or temple or mosque – complex liturgies or simple personal rituals – is aimed at reinforcing faith, the sense of the ultimate meaning of things, in a particularly graphic and personal way. This may be intended to inspire a sense that God has a special care, even a particular love, for the worshipper. Equally it may inspire awe and even dread – a dire warning of the wrath of

87

God. The symbols of faith work on the imagination, leading the individual to recognize a special relationship with God, who is perceived not as distant but at the centre of one's world and, one might almost say, at the heart of one's 'true self'.

The Spirituality of Devotion

How does this type of spirituality differ from that associated with ritual? The latter evokes faith through a liturgical celebration of the great symbols; the worshipper takes the initiative in making a formal submission in obedience to the Divine. The former seems much more concerned to stress that the initiative lies with God, that what is built up is a relationship of loving response to God's prior act of self-giving. In Indian religion this is the spirituality associated with *bhakti*. The word comes from a root meaning to 'share in', and with its connotations of becoming attached to someone can almost be translated 'loyalty'. What is implied is the mutual acceptance and trust of two people who commit themselves to each other. God is perceived in personal terms as the one who enters into a dialogue with human beings. In the history of Indian religion I noted how *jñana-yoga* with its meditative and mystical practices developed to a great extent in reaction to the ritualism of *karma-yoga*. In fact the former can be as élitist as the latter – which is one reason why this third form of spirituality, *bhakti-yoga*, made its appearance on the Indian scene. *Bhakti* is the spirituality of the devotee, the one who participates in the life of God by recognizing and sharing in God's all-dominating, all-encompassing activity. The many forms of *bhakti*-religion, from passionate devotion to one of the great gods, Vishnu or Śiva, to a special relationship established with a particular god in order to enjoy some favour, all depend on a sense of the divine initiative. Though taking on much of the style and form of *karma* and *jñana*, the way of devotion is unique in recognizing fully the extent to which spirituality has the character of response. Prayer is not so much action as reaction: an acknowledgement that *God's* action is always prior.

To recognize and respond to the signs of divine action demands a willingness to be led. 'You did not choose me, but I chose you', as Jesus said to his disciples (John 15.16). To be chosen, and to be led, can sometimes be rough experiences. Too easily we interpret beneficence in terms of indulgence. Indian religion immediately calls such assumptions into question: for every picture of Krishna, the lovable but mischievous child who steals his mother's butter-milk, there are as many of Kali, the 'dark one', the goddess of blood and gore who devours her enemies. Alongside Rama, the stout warrior vanquishing the demon king, Ravana, must be set Śiva the destroyer. And yet the great majority of Hindus are *bhaktas*, devo-tees of a particular form of the Lord, Bhagavan, who for them rep-resents the Divine immanent in creation. The image of the Lord at the heart of the temple or the home dominates their lives and – in a sometimes quite mysterious way – brings a strength and con-solation quite unknown in our other two types of spirituality.

Such ambivalent images of God present the Christian, used to a God revealed as the loving Father of Jesus Christ, with some-thing of a problem. How can God be portrayed in such a form? Surely if God is all-good and all-loving there can be no place for the darkness of Kali or the malevolence of Śiva? This is not the place to get into metaphysical discussions about the nature of evil. My subject is, rather, the use of imagery and symbols in Christian and Indian spirituality. Here I would want to make two prelimi-nary observations. The first is that devotion can all too easily be re-duced to an empty ritual of reliance on a soft-hearted deity. God may be turned into an indulgent granny-figure who allows herself to be besieged by whining children desperate for goodies. Such love is cheap. It costs nothing and proves nothing. Neither the granny nor the children are forced to change or to grow. Similarly the image of God which emerges from so much uncritical or fun-damentalist Christianity ends up with a spirituality which is intro-spective and self-satisfied. The God revealed in Jesus the 'personal Lord and Saviour' may be no more than a sort of private chum who strikes up a buddy-buddy relationship which can become totally exclusive. As with the granny there is no problem in manipulating such a God. The power of love is emasculated.

Connected with this is a second point. We should note the role that such pictures play in the telling of a story, particularly a story which is supposed in some way to give an insight into the way things really are. However we are to understand Kali and Śiva, it is not by reducing them to devils and their cult to that of demon-worship. The fearsome goddess is engaged in a battle with the forces of darkness, a battle which is going on all the time and in which the devotee is inevitably – and sometimes painfully – caught up. Myths mirror life and its awful ambiguities. Life is not ordered or exact; even when we think we have it under control, disaster strikes. Rainstorms disrupt cricket matches and dash expectations of victory; commuters find themselves at the mercy of broken-down escalators and decrepit signalling-systems. At a less trivial level, death cuts down a vigorous executive in the prime of life; a child dies from leukaemia. Stories, symbols and metaphors help us to understand an inevitably disordered and dangerous existence, to lead us into an intuitive appreciation of what cannot be stated with precision and exactness.

This is not to reject the attempts of philosophers to answer what is often called the 'problem of evil'. It is simply to underline the fact that when we move into the area represented by spirituality or religious practice we find that people are not looking for philosophically coherent answers. In fact, if Hindu *bhakti* is anything to go by, the more open-ended the metaphors the more they are capable of supporting the devotee. Like the cross, Kali is a sign of contradiction, a question mark which warns against the danger or reducing the reality of the Divine to an image of our own making. There is more to the practice of religion than an exercise in rationality.

These points take us into the heart of the way of devotion – into its beauty and its paradox. That the relationship between God and humankind should be described in terms of obedience or knowledge, as with the two 'ways' or forms of spirituality which we have already examined, is not difficult to understand. But what sense does it make to speak of a relationship of 'loyalty' or of God 'loving' us? Is such language not too anthropomorphic, reducing God to a human level, subject to all the complexities, the emotions, the jealousies, which are part and parcel of human loving?

The reply that for a Christian this is all implied in the great covenant themes of the Bible and in the supreme mystery of the incarnation of Christ is no solution. Of course the incarnation, as much as the death and resurrection, of Christ reveals a God of love; so much is this the case that John can say that 'God is love' (1John 4.8,16) and 'God so loved the world that he sent his only Son' (John 3.16). It is, however, too easy to take such a truth for granted, to fail to recognize what is implied in the revelation of a God who is love. The first time that two people discover that they love each other is as much a self-revelation as it is a revelation of the other; in other words they discover through the encounter not just that they are capable of giving love but worthy of receiving it, that they are *lovable*. This is by no means obvious. Most of us, if we are honest, have great difficulty in accepting that we are worthy of the unconditional esteem and respect of another – for that is what love implies. Such is our insecurity that we think we have to earn that respect, that we are always in danger of losing it. Christianity is founded on the truth that God offers an unconditional love, and that in Christ God goes to extraordinary lengths to prove it, but it may take a lifetime to recognize the fact. The problem is recognizing the deepest implications of that statement: 'God is love.' It is this truth which the spirituality of devotion seeks to explore, leading people of faith from equanimity and openness, the fruits of the undistracted way of *jñana*, to a realization of what it really means to love and to be loved, the fruits of *bhakti*.

Love Seeking Understanding

When *bhakti* makes its first appearance in Indian religion it is still cast very much in the language represented by *jñana-yoga*; the aim, as in the various forms of meditation mentioned earlier, is to 'know' the truth about reality and thus to gain the experience of *moksha* or release. *Bhakti* is primarily to be developed as a means to an end; the emotions are subjected to the quest for knowledge. Later, however, there develops a different sort of *bhakti*, one which takes a variety of different forms, but – to generalize somewhat – gives much more weight to the value of the emotions *as such*, particularly to the emotion of love. So much of contemporary Hinduism is dominated by devotional cults which stress total reliance on God – even in moments of dereliction and despair. The devotee discards all 'techniques' and appears as he or she truly is: beset by sin and doubt, yet trusting in the promise and grace of God.

This, then, is to repeat that the spirituality of *bhakti* centres on the quality of response to the divine initiative. A certain shift of emphasis from activity to passivity can be discerned – a process which is mirrored in the development of *bhakti-yoga* in Indian religion. The first stage is to be found in the greatest of all Hindu scriptures, the Bhagavad Gita, the Song of the Lord. In one of the classic images of Indian religion the god Krishna appears as the charioteer of the young warrior Arjuna and teaches him about the way in which religious faith is to be used to cope with the anxieties and inevitable conflicts caused by living in an ambiguous world. Arjuna's particular problem is about his coming engagement in a bloody war – not, perhaps, an everyday occurrence. Nevertheless the lessons of the Gita are as relevant today as when they were first taught some two and a half thousand years ago.

The Gita is not just a compendium of practical wisdom. It centres round an extraordinary vision which Krishna grants to the young warrior. This revelation of Krishna's heavenly form, more properly an apocalyptic explosion, full of light, colour and energy, is scarcely guaranteed to provoke love in the heart of the clearly rather frightened Arjuna. In fact in many ways it fits uneasily into the 'logic' of the teaching of the Gita. Krishna's aim is to impress on Arjuna that the only way to reconcile all the conflicting demands of a busy and divided life is to keep his mind fixed on the Lord. Krishna is the example *par excellence* of the yogic ideal of 'desireless action'. Life can only be lived with some measure of equanimity if Arjuna manages to achieve a sort of detached obedience by fixing his mind on Krishna. Thus he can get on with the task in hand without worrying about the long-term results. In some ways the method of prayer – for that is what is being taught – is a simple exercise of attaching the mind to Krishna. 'Let him sit,' says the god, 'integrated, intent on Me: for firmly established is that man's wisdom whose senses are subdued' (2.61). *Bhakti*, 'loyalty', is a form of the yogic practice of fixing the senses on the image or icon of Krishna so that one may gain wisdom and insight.

But what results from this action of attaching oneself to the image of God? At the end of the Gita the real revelation takes place. Krishna tells Arjuna that 'You are dear to me'. God is not a remote source of power and glory. God is love. This is the real source of 'desireless action': the knowledge that we are loved, that God has taken the initiative to love us and asks for our loving devotion in return. Hence the appropriateness of translating the word *bhakti* as loyalty, with its sense of remaining faithful and dedicating oneself to the service of another.

The Love Which Endures All Things

The Gita is without a doubt the best-loved of all Indian scriptures, but its importance lies less in its mass appeal than in the fact that it stands at the head of the extraordinary development of Indian devotional religion. The figure of Krishna, a confident and ever-so-reasonable guru in the Gita, attaches to himself a rich mythology which focuses on his childish pranks, his love-affairs with the cow-maidens and his never-ending attempts to induce in his devotees an ecstatic and emotional response to his loving advances. Krishna, balanced on one foot playing the flute, is as familiar as Śiva Nataraja, the 'Lord of the Dance', arms and legs flying in a circle of flame. Krishna seems at first sight to present few problems: the irresistible youthful lover stands clearly as a metaphor for the overwhelming love of God for the human soul. But in the tenth-century CE poem, the Bhagavata Purana, the full complexity of the divine love-affair is graphically presented.

At dead of night Krishna entices the cow-maidens out of their houses to dance with him in the moonlight. And to show how much he loves them he multiplies his form so that each one thinks she alone is dancing with the beloved. Then, however, comes the agony of separation. Krishna disappears and the cow-maidens are left stricken to the heart, pining for the absent god who seems to have deserted them. All they have left are their memories – and the words and symbols which conjure the memories. All they can do is call on the god to return while – paradoxically – nursing their sense of absence as the only sign of his presence.

It would be difficult to find many parallels to this highly emotional, heavily anthropomorphized, vision of the God of love in the scriptures of the prophetic religions. Beside the largely strait-laced spirituality which dominates the legal and prophetic books of the Hebrew Bible there is only the occasional glimpse of intense passion – for example, in the sensuous Song of Songs. Here God is the subject of a turbulent love-affair: 'Upon my bed by night I sought him whom my soul loves; I sought him, but found him not; I called him, but he gave no answer.' The desperate search gives way a little later to the ecstasy of lovers reunited: 'I found him whom my heart loves. I held him, and would not let him go until I had brought him into my mother's house, and into the chamber of her that conceived me' (Song 3.1–4). Such frankness may be exceptional in the Bible, where much of the imagery associated with the God of love is set in a more traditionally controlled mode: the guidance of the shepherd (Ps. 23), the care of the mother hen (Luke 13.34). But what are we to make of the deeply moving mystical writings of Eckhart and John of the Cross, Teresa of Avila and the unknown author of *The Cloud of Unknowing*? This is love-mysticism of the highest order – the relationship with God expressed with all the emotion of joy and pain, discovery and loss, union and separation which true love knows only too well.

This may seem a long way from the spirituality of devotion but, just as there is a continuity between the more intellectual mode of *bhakti* in the Gita and the emotionalism of later scriptures like the Bhagavata Purana, so there is in prophetic religion. In the Judaism of the Hebrew Bible, for instance, there is no end to the images and stories which try to encapsulate the experience of the pain of loving. Once we try to understand the divine-human relationship in terms of love, rather than knowledge, everything – even disaster – can be seen as an aspect of the great love-affair between God and his people. When evil strikes it is interpreted as the punishment God inflicts on his people for their lack of response – Saul for his faithlessness, David for his adultery. Such a love is never obvious in its purpose. What, for instance, are we to make of the God who permits Satan, 'the adversary', to test Job by subjecting him to physical and mental torment? 'Behold,' says the Lord to Satan, 'he is in your power; only spare his life' (Job 2.6). Satan seems here to represent some sort of divine agency: God remains in control, acting through a mediator – though it remains a strange way of acting. How do we understand such a vision? Job listens with scant attention to the specious arguments and short-sighted rationalizing of his friends. They completely fail to understand God's purposes. From the testing of Job comes a new strength, but – more important – God's sovereign power to act and to judge in sometimes mysterious and incomprehensible ways is emphasized and safeguarded.

In some ways Job's experience can be seen as a sort of 'dark night of the soul'. His is the classic story of undeserved suffering. However much he is told that he must have done something dreadful to incur God's anger he insists on his innocence. There is no 'logic' behind what has happened, no appeal to moral failure which can justify such disaster. In the end he knows that his patience, his faith and loyalty to God, will be vindicated. 'For I know that my Redeemer lives, and at last he will stand upon the earth; and after my skin has been thus destroyed, then from my flesh I shall see God' (Job 19.25–6). All Job can rely on to sustain him through this crisis of loss and loneliness is the memory of the love of God which used to sustain him and which he knows can never die.

This is the heart of Job's faith, the conviction that God cannot change and that nothing he has done warrants any change in the attitude of God towards him. Such is the mystery of the divine-human relationship. Suffering is inevitable, not because it is deserved – an appropriate punishment meted out to those who have offended the all-righteous God – but because the whole of life is suffering once one has been removed, even for a short while, out of that conscious awareness of the loving presence of God. Job had once basked in God's blessings but, once taken from the tangible enjoyment of that love, nothing, least of all the conventionally pious arguments of his friends, can console him.

The Response of the Heart

Here we come up against a crucial difference between devotion and our other two types of spirituality. Of course, there are plenty of similarities. Devotion, as much as liturgical prayer or meditation, is a spiritual exercise; it needs to be *done*. In most religions worship requires immense amounts of preparation. Meditation, too, has spawned a vast literature of techniques. Devotional prayer may have more of a spontaneous character, but more often than not it focuses on traditional forms – rosaries, short mantras, prayers before images and statues. To some extent devotion is based, like meditation, on the concept of the personal ritual: the pilgrims to the great shrines in Jerusalem are going through a time-honoured round of practices. But why *do* anything at all? With our first two types of spirituality the answer is fairly clear: a certain formality is demanded by the concept of the divine-human relationship implied in the prayer itself. *Bhakti* religion, on the other hand, lacks formality; the image, and the memories and emotions which the image evokes, are all that matters. Poetry, hymns and prayers can certainly be developed as the 'techniques' of this type of prayer, but are strictly unnecessary. All that really matters is the level of emotional response, the response of the heart.

In the final analysis this depends less on what is 'done' than on what we allow 'to be done' in us. *Jñana-yoga* begins in faith and leads to a certain passive quality, the act of waiting before the Divine Mystery. *Bhakti-yoga* begins in the same way, but causes faith to grow through the use of images and symbols which mirror the divine-human relationship, the response to the divine initiative –

whether this is represented as a passionate longing for God the divine lover or, at the other end of the scale, in a sort of resigned acquiescence, an acceptance of the darkness and distance from God which is portrayed in the figure of Job or the image of Kali.

CHAPTER 8

Images of Human Perfection

The master spoke to Ma-tsu.
'Why are you sitting in meditation?'
'In order to become a Buddha.'
The master took up a tile and started polishing it.
'What are you doing?' asked Ma-tsu.
'Polishing this stone in order to make a mirror.'
Ma-tsu looked puzzled.
'But how can you make a mirror out of a tile?'
'How can you make a Buddha by sitting in meditation?'

There is no doubt that some forms of spiritual practice, for example Yoga and relaxation techniques like Transcendental Meditation, can enrich the quality of life, whether this is seen in terms of enhancing a particular potential or, in more negative terms, in order to overcome stress. Various examples could be cited. I remember, for instance, that the first Yoga class I ever held was attended by the school rugby team. I have to admit that it came as something of a disappointment to me to realize that they were not guided by the pure, disinterested desire for knowledge, still less for spiritual refreshment. Yoga became an extension of their already considerable physical culture. Whether their results that season owed anything to my instruction I shall never know. Nor does it matter. My consolation lay in knowing that I had managed to pass on something of my fundamental opinion that success in most walks of life – even and perhaps especially in sport – depends on keeping mental and physical carefully integrated.

This in itself is no bad thing. But what do we mean by 'success' and how do we go about measuring it? I have tried to point to the problems which can arise when any one form of spirituality is used in complete isolation from the others. If there is a problem with the way of devotion it lies in what can become an exaggerated individualism, a concern with *my* relationship with God, *my* prayer, *my* personal experience. But the same can apply to the way of meditative prayer too. Is it not just one more manifestation of the Western obsession with the individual self? Spiritual practices from the East are dragged into service as self-improvement techniques, subordinated to the demands of the enterprise culture, of getting on and keeping up. No person of faith can view such reductionism with equanimity – least of all those committed to the vision of Ultimate Truth and Value contained in the various yogic and devotional traditions of India.

There is clearly no reason why Yoga practices should not be adapted for specific ends; indeed this is precisely what happened in India. But what are we to make of an approach to spirituality which puts the development or perfection of the individual ego or self at the centre of experience? The true purpose of spirituality is to express a relationship with whatever is considered to be the Ultimate. A narrow obsession with 'technique' – as I have tried to show – runs the risk of trivializing that purpose. Whatever we mean by 'success', it cannot be seen in such narrowly pragmatic terms as finishing a task successfully or winning the game – even when the metaphor becomes somewhat clichéd as the 'great game of life'.

Losing Oneself

In an earlier chapter I devoted some time to presenting the Buddhist Middle Way in order to illustrate the point – present in some way in all the great religions – that, whatever we mean by perfection, it only comes through death to self. This is to be accomplished not through ascetical training but through a contemplative equanimity which (in Christian terms) allows God, the source of all harmony, to work in our lives. In other words the focus of attention is shifted from self to the radical 'otherness' of the Ultimate. What, then, becomes of self? What sense is to be made of the paradox of Jesus that 'whoever would save his life will lose it, but whoever loses his life for my sake will find it' (Matt. 16.25)?

What I have called the 'Western obsession with the individual self' probably owes more to a tradition of philosophizing associated with Descartes and Kant than it does to its biblical roots. Nevertheless Christians can be forgiven for thinking of the human person in terms of the 'autonomous ego'. In the New Testament Paul develops a number of images to describe the Christian life:

putting on armour, running the race, pressing towards the goal. Despite (or is it because of?) his celebrated teaching on justification by faith in the epistle to the Romans he gives us an enormous amount of moral exhortation. To some extent he is only spelling out the consequences of faith for Christian living. Answering some very specific questions and dealing with particular communities he knew well, he is saying that if you believe such and such then you must behave in an appropriate manner. Pressure, sometimes not so gentle, is put on people to react to what God has revealed of himself in the death and resurrection of Christ and, through their actions, to become a particular sort of person.

Paul's rhetoric, however, has been universalized by the Church into a type of moral asceticism. What people are worth is measured in terms of what they do. Christian living becomes a matter of performing certain actions which show that the will, subject to sinful inclinations, has been overcome. Such a focus on the importance of proving oneself tends to obscure the wonderful vision Paul presents of the Spirit of God acting in human hearts. Once the passages of moral exhortation are properly understood, however, the ascetical spirit they have spawned can be put in context. The gospel is Good News not because it teaches standards of behaviour which God expects (the law taught that), but because it proclaims God's salvation to those who fail to come up to those standards. The gospel which many Christians have heard stresses the first point, the ideals of human perfection and harmony, but ignores the second, the reconciling love of God which makes such perfection *possible*.

No life, not even that of the most committed Christian, is led totally in the light. The effects of sin remain. Faith is often severely tested by events beyond one's control and no amount of moral exhortation will make any difference. In fact too much exhortation may only make matters worse, turning Paul's 'striving upward for the prize' into nothing more than a guilt-trip. Paul's perspective, however, emphasizes what the Spirit of God is in process of creating – a renewed humanity. The truth revealed in the gospel is the new life in the Spirit of Christ. Human sin, weakness and failure still oppress but are not the end. 'If Christ is in you,' says Paul to the Romans,

> although your bodies are dead because of sin, your spirits are alive because of righteousness. If the Spirit of him who raised Jesus ... dwells in you, he who raised Christ Jesus from the dead will give life

to your mortal bodies also through his Spirit which dwells in you. (Rom. 8.10–11).

Salvation and Human Perfection

Actually to live this perspective is not easy. It is hardly surprising if the Good News has been interpreted simply as a call to repentance. Some of the sayings of Jesus make enormous demands. In the Sermon on the Mount, for instance, he says 'You ... must be perfect, as your heavenly Father is perfect' (Matt. 5.48). Elsewhere he says that 'No one who puts his hand to the plough and looks back is fit for the kingdom of God' (Luke 9.62) and 'how hard it is to enter the kingdom of God' (Mark 10.24). It sounds like moral exhortation, but the context teaches otherwise. The last quotation comes from the story of the rich man. When faced with the ultimate demand, to give up everything and come back and follow Jesus, the man turns away, 'for he had great possessions' (Mark 10.22). This is the lead-in to the ensuing conversation. When the astonished disciples expostulate with the question 'Then who can be saved?', Jesus replies by saying: 'With men it is impossible, but not with God; for all things are possible with God' (Mark 10.27). As long as the disciples rely on their own strength, their own ability to respond to God's invitation, they are bound to fail. But God can work miracles in those who submit in faith and *allow themselves* to be changed. The problem is, of course, that the disciples – or, at any rate, those who, like the rich man, thought they had to do it all themselves – first have to admit their weakness if God is to be their strength. Paul's wonderful ascetical metaphors only make sense as a response to, not a preparation for, the transforming work of God's Holy Spirit.

This may give some idea of what is meant by dying to self – at least in Christian terms: I become a person only by acknowledging my creatureliness, my utter dependence on God. That said, images of perfection abound in Christianity. Unlike Buddhists, who subordinate the teacher to the teaching, Christians fix their attention on Christ, who is *both* teacher *and* teaching. Christ is no less than the perfect image of humanity, the example and the ideal: the one who, by entering into a loving relationship with the God he describes as Father, holds out to all people, even the weakest, the possibility of growing into the fullness of what it is to be human. A proper awareness of dependence leaves room for the Spirit to work. As the Lord says to Paul when he asks to be relieved of his 'thorn in the flesh', 'My grace is sufficient for you, for my power is made perfect in weakness' (2 Cor. 12.9).

Naturally it is impossible to give here an adequate account of the Christian theology of salvation. Not only are we dealing with a variety of metaphors, the 'stuff' of theology, each of which contains its own nuances of meaning – the language, for instance, of deification, redemption, enlightenment or atonement – but, beyond the introductory remarks above, which as it were 'set the scene', the scriptural material is notoriously difficult to summarize, let alone evaluate. Is salvation present or future, collective or individual? What is the role of Christ? What do we expect Christ to do for us?

Theologies of salvation are rightly fluid but, in general, tend in one of two directions: recognizing either Christ as the Saviour who is 'the way, and the truth, and the life', leading people to the Father, or the Father as the Saviour who incorporates them into the life-giving death and resurrection of his Son. In each one there is an agent and an agency, one who acts and a mode of action. To some extent both must remain utterly mysterious. Christians confess their belief in 'our Lord and Saviour Jesus Christ' who died 'for our salvation' but are not tied to any particular theology of the mechanism by which salvation can be said to be effective in their lives. Christ is clearly central to the interpretation of Christian experience – even if different theologies of the Mystery of Christ and the action of the Spirit are possible. Other faiths do not speak of Christ in such terms, but they do echo the Christian's desire for salvation or human fulfilment. In understanding the human condition – both its need of and possibility for perfection – a dialogue with Indian religion is particularly enriching.

What Makes a Person?

What do the mystical religions of India make of the quest for human perfection? There is a famous story about a missionary who was sent out to a distant Far Eastern land to convert the pagans. Being a zealous man, he decided he ought to get to know the local religion and duly set off in search of suitable natives. Eventually he came across a Buddhist monk, clothed in his saffron robes, seated under a tree. 'Tell me,' said the missionary, 'who are you praying to?' 'I am praying to no one,' said the Buddhist after a short pause. 'Well, what is the name of your God?' asked the missionary. 'There is no God,' came the reply. 'Then what is your prayer about?' pleaded the missionary. 'There is no prayer,' said the monk. The missionary was by this stage somewhat bewildered and turned to go away. As he was retreating, the Buddhist called after him, 'Oh, and by the way, there is no one praying either.'

Apocryphal or not, the story is instructive. Buddhism is deliberately self-effacing. It is not dominated by priests and patriarchs, still less by glowering ayatollahs. The greatest of its personalities refused to establish any sort of hierarchy, leaving his followers with the *dharma* alone to guide their steps on the Way. Naturally enough dominant figures emerged – the Buddha's immediate disciples, Ananda and Mahakaśyapa, Nagarjuna, the great exponent of the Madhyamika philosophy, Bodhidharma, the legendary founder of Zen, and so many others right down to the Dalai Lama. Under their influence Buddhism has developed and grown in many different directions. Theravada follows much the same practice in the different countries of South East Asia where it is the dominant religion, but is far from homogeneous. The title Mahayana much more obviously covers a multitude of schools, each with particular versions and adaptations of an original vision of the nature of human life. The extent to which that original can be reconstructed is not our concern. In all of them is to be found a sense of the original spirit – whether we are speaking of the conservative calm of the Theravadin forest-dwelling hermit or the almost anarchical good humour of the Tibetan tantric *siddha* or 'accomplished one'. As we have already noted, the Way is adapted to different cultural needs and circumstances, but for all the true guide or teacher is the Way itself. The influence of individual personalities cannot be discounted in Buddhism any more than the interests of the four evangelists can be excised from the 'pure gospel' of Jesus. Nevertheless, in the Buddhist tradition, as in the Christian, it is possible to discern the key points of teaching about the human person which guide the many schools of interpretation.

In what is traditionally called the first sermon, the Buddha speaks of the human person as made up of five material and psychological factors, all of which are rigorously analysed as subject to suffering. To the question What makes a person? there is only one answer: What is given in experience. And human experience is the experience of suffering, impermanence and insubstantiality, the 'lack of soul or self'. To realize this truth, to become enlightened, requires years of arduous moral and meditative training. In the Theravada tradition the meditation on the body in ten stages of decomposition is still taught. Meditation in the local cemetery is a thing of the past, but in one training centre that I visited in Colombo I came across appropriately nauseous illustrations painted round the wall of the meditation hall. Looking not unlike posters for the worst kind of cheap horror movie, they are intended in the first place to inspire a certain revulsion against all forms of lust and sensuality, but they are also graphic illustrations of the Buddha's own analysis of the human condition. My guide said they were not often used, but on our way out he opened a cupboard at the end of a long corridor. There hung the skeleton of a monk who had died meditating in the forest. 'The young monks find this much more satisfactory,' he said. The aim is simple: to bring home the truth that in this body there is only suffering – nothing that may be considered permanent. There is no 'soul' or 'spirit' somehow hiding behind the elements we experience, nor – to change the metaphor – is there anything which holds them all together.

Clearly such a position presents many problems – philosophical as well as emotional. To deny the existence of a substantive and permanent person goes counter to basic human instincts, and remains a controversial aspect of Buddhist teaching. Even in the earliest days there were those who objected to *anatmavada* – the 'teaching of no self' – and various revisions of what is certainly a radical doctrine have occurred since. It cannot be doubted, however, that the mainstream of Buddhist tradition holds the position which denies the existence of a substantial self. What does it mean to say that 'there is no one praying either'? The first move, as always, is to establish the context. The Buddha is not attacking common sense, but criticizing certain current philosophical and religious notions about what it means to be a person. Thus the first task is to look at the relationship between individual and society – in short, the attitude to caste.

Persons in Society

Today, of course, what seems to have begun as a relatively straightforward system of four classes has developed into a luxuriant hierarchy of castes and sub-castes which defies analysis. No account of Hinduism would be complete without some reference to the way in which caste dominates every aspect of Indian life – and modes of thought. Inevitably caste affects all the religions which have originated in India. And that must include Buddhism. At least in its ideal form, caste-society has a place for everyone, each co-operating in the building of the whole. The principle is that described in an ancient Vedic hymn known as the Hymn of the Primeval Person. Here the universe is depicted as a huge male figure: 'His mouth is the *brahmin*, his arms the warrior, his two thighs the merchant, his feet the servant' (*Rig Veda* 10.90). This cosmic person gives us a picture of a stratified society in which everyone is ranked hierarchically. There is no such thing as an individual person outside the system; to be a person with an identity you have to belong within the system, as a member of a caste. And to belong to a caste is a matter of birth: *brahmins* are born not made.

The Buddha confronted a system which displayed many obvious weaknesses. The *brahmins*, as the head of the hierarchy and thus embodying its ideals and values, felt reasonably at home in the world – for it was a world which they controlled. It was not in their interests to change the social system as such, but it did, of course, suit them to adapt the rituals and liturgies which were the source of their authority. Liturgy, as we have already noted, is an end in itself; it is self-justifying. But it is only effective as long as it provides for people's security. In a time of rapid social change it was almost inevitable that the ritual would become more obscure and less capable of satisfying people's religious aspirations. For the Buddha the social system which maintained such a power-structure was morally and religiously corrupting. Not only did it fail to provide answers to questions people asked about the next life, it failed to sustain them in their battle to survive this one.

The major criticisms, however, were reserved for the way of thinking which it encouraged. This presumed an intrinsic superiority for the *brahmin* élite – that to be born a *brahmin* was automatically to be a learned and virtuous person. In other words the *brahmins* confused social status with moral worth. Traditionally there are said to be five typical marks of the true *brahmin*: noble birth, learning, beauty, virtue and wisdom. In one conversation Buddha shows that only the last two are essential and that they are to be found in the way of life which he preaches – an ideal which can be reached by anyone who perseveres on the Middle Way.

Thus wisdom and virtue are the fruits of the ascetical path, not the exclusive preserve of one particular caste. Elsewhere the point is made more strongly: the true *brahmin*, a 'seer whose vision is pure', lives a 'life of pure heroism', and 'in perfection is one with Supreme Perfection'. Now if this is social revolution then it is all very subtle. What is Buddha driving at?

Taking Responsibility

The point to note is that he does not reject the term *brahmin* but changes its application to include all who strive for perfection according to the way he teaches. The ideals of wisdom and virtue are accepted and praised but they are not the preserve of one social group within the system; they belong to the group *as a whole*. The purpose of the caste-system is not to serve the vested interests of the superior caste in the hierarchy; rather, if everyone fulfils those particular tasks and functions which have been assigned to them by birth by co-operating with each other, virtue and wisdom can be preserved and attained by everyone. The trouble is that there is never proper co-operation. The caste-system, like every other system of social organization, is riddled with human limitations. The Buddha's aim, therefore, is to criticize the excesses of the existing system, not to replace it with another. And whatever his strictures on the caste-system, it should be noted that Buddha did not reject the essential truth it taught: no one lives independent of others. Enlightenment can never come from the selfish pursuit of individual perfection.

This immediately takes us back to the Buddha's teaching of 'no-self'. To be a person means, in the first place, to take charge of one's own life, to realize that one is not condemned by a capricious fate to lead an existence over which one has no control. Thus the first demand of Buddhist life, the first of the 'three trainings', is moral responsibility. There is no external authority, no code of conduct, which the individual does not agree to accept by a personal commitment. This is the first stage in becoming a person: accepting the demands of a moral life lived with other moral beings in society.

The objection is that even the moral life can be thoroughly self-indulgent if the only reason I take it on is to fulfil the first requirement of making progress on the Way. It is true that Buddhist teaching demands moral responsibility in order to attain purity of action; only the sincere and upright can reach enlightenment. In which case, is not the moral life just another form of vested self-interest, differing only from the *brahmin* in that the Buddhist has an eye on future enlightenment whereas the *brahmin* is concerned to preserve present power? Such an argument forgets that Buddhism teaches three central elements, three 'trainings', which all interact: morality, meditation and wisdom. Morality is not a means to attain wisdom; morality is the practice of wisdom. Thus, the Buddha would argue, just as one cannot be truly wise without acting morally, so acting morally is impossible without wisdom, seeing things correctly, as they are. To put it in terms of the Noble Eightfold Path, Right View implies Right Action and vice versa in the same way that – as we noted in speaking of meditation – Right Effort is moderated by the practice of Right Mindfulness.

The Interdependence of All

If there is one key insight which this doctrine is seeking to teach it is the interrelatedness of all things and all beings. Again and again we find the teaching of the Buddha taking us back to the central demand to acknowledge *dharma*, to see things as they really are: dependent on one another. The human person, the experiencing subject, is no more the centre of the universe than the *brahmin* is the sole justification of the entire hierarchy of castes. Whatever we understand by human perfection, it is not to be achieved by establishing oneself as an individual who exists apart from, still less dominates, society. In the Theravada tradition the 'true *brahmin*' is distinguished by wisdom and virtue. Later, in the Mahayana tradition the marks of the *bodhisattva* are spelt out in terms of a series of perfections; the fullest version gives ten – generosity, discipline, patience, will-power, meditation, wisdom, method, vows, strength and knowledge. The path to enlightenment consists less in the practice of the abstract Eightfold Path and much more in the imitation of the Buddha, who shows through his life what it means to be – and *act as* – an enlightened one.

This is not to say, however, that the two traditions are at odds in their account of human perfection. Whatever the nuances of interpretation – and they are many – the ideal is not the lonely silent sage of popular myth. The perfectly enlightened one preaches wisdom out of compassion for the welfare of all 'sentient beings'. The doctrine of 'no-self', so often understood negatively and interpreted as the ultimate expression of Buddhist nihilism, is intended to develop a sense similar to what I spoke of earlier, in Christian terms, as 'creatureliness': no individual has any substantial existence apart from all others. In this sense there is 'no *one* praying'.

A Successful Person?

What, then, is a person? Buddhism and Christianity come at the question with very different presuppositions. The Buddha is opposed to all forms of constructive metaphysics which attempt to locate Ultimate Reality in a particular experience. Teaching is intended to be practical, helping people to make progress on the Way. Thus he gives us a critique of religiosity in general and of the religion of the *brahmin* élite in particular. The so-called Unanswered Questions – the nature of the world, enlightenment and the human self – are intended to direct the meditator away from an attachment to wrong views which can be as disturbing internally as noise and constant activity can be distracting externally. Right View acknowledges the First Noble Truth, which in its fuller form as the three marks of reality – suffering, impermanence and insubstantiality, or 'Lack of Self' – states that the root cause of all attachment is the misguided belief that the individual ego has some sort of substantial existence or 'self'. The Buddha's analysis of the human person into the 'five aggregates' – form, sensations, perceptions, mental states and consciousness – is intended to exhaust all possible items of experience. No substantial entity, no unchanging person, is to be found. The way of meditation called mindfulness identifies experience for what it is and recognizes that there can be no permanent duration of any of the aspects of the human person. In Buddhist terms, to speak of personality, self, or ego – the 'separateness of things' – is just to use a mode of speech.

There is, however, a similar understanding of the aim of this 'spiritual strategy'. Christians will be able to accept it to the extent that it reinforces their equally paradoxical insistence that the life of the Spirit only comes through dying to self. To recognize the limits of language and the extent to which one's vision of reality is coloured by a capacity for projection is the object of Buddhist meditation – and therefore of Buddhism as a whole. The doctrine of 'no-self' has an essential truth-function, without which the intellectual edifice of Buddhism would have no coherence. As with its correlate, the teaching about *nirvana*, the ultimate value of the doctrine of 'no-self' cannot be categorized. What both doctrines do is to point the practitioner in a certain direction; they make for a method by which salvation can be achieved. To put it another way, 'doctrine' in Buddhism is the formal structure of Right View without which progress on the Way cannot be made. Certain assumptions – that there is an 'other-worldly' reality which is where we 'go' after death or that there is an essential soul or self to be 'discovered within' – are questioned.

I started by asking what we mean by 'success' in the spiritual life. Perhaps this is another of the Buddha's Unanswered Questions and the correct response is to keep silence. Certainly we need to be careful of the categories we use and note the presuppositions with which we begin. For Buddhist meditation, just as much as for Christian prayer, notions of success or even progress seem strangely inappropriate. That faith deepens, that prayer and meditation become easier, that struggles are overcome, that a certain peace results – all this is clear and much to be welcomed. But in the end, all expectations, even the most minimal, must be put to one side in favour of a simple openness to Ultimate Mystery – or, to put it in deliberately paradoxical terms, a sort of 'active' or 'positive' *waiting*.

This is the Buddhist experience which, as the little Zen story at the head of this chapter teaches, is as much about recognizing the folly of human ambition as it is about striving to realize human potential. But there is also something profoundly Christian here: not just the serene acceptance of impermanence and weakness, but the joyful patience which contemplates the mystery of God.

Hakuin, the greatest master of the Rinzai school of Zen, tells another story. 'A man', he says,

> went astray and arrived at a spot which had never been travelled by the foot of man. Before him there yawned a bottomless chasm. His feet stood on the slippery moss of a rock and no secure foothold appeared around him. He could step neither forward nor backward. Only death awaited him. The vine which he grasped with his left hand and the tendril which he held with his right could offer him little help. His life hung as by a single thread. Were he to release both his hands at once, his dry bones would come to nought.

This is the human condition. Somewhat bleakly put, it is true, but sublimely realistic. Hakuin goes on to talk about the way that the *koan*, those obscure little verbal puzzles, are used to focus attention on the paradox of life itself – which one must live with patience and which can only be resolved in the stillness of inner recollection. Once the restlessness occasioned by that senseless striving for 'success' has been quietened, a 'waiting' which is yet 'active' and alive can begin. Hakuin concludes that the Zen disciple

> comes to a point where his mind is as if dead and his will as if extinguished. This state is like a wide void over a deep chasm and no hold remains for hand or foot. All thoughts vanish and in his bosom burns hot anxiety. But then suddenly it occurs that with the *koan* both body and mind break. This is the instant when his hands are released over the abyss. In this sudden upsurge it is as if one drinks water and knows for oneself hot and cold. Great joy wells up. This is called rebirth [in the Pure Land]. This is termed seeing into one's nature. Everything depends on pushing forward and not doubting that with the help of this concentration one will eventually penetrate to the ground of one's nature.[1]

Note

1 Quoted in Heinrich Dumoulin, *A History of Zen Buddhism* (London: Faber & Faber, 1963), p. 259.

CHAPTER 9
The Activity of Compassion

This is to be done by one skilful in seeking the good, having attained to that tranquil state of calm: let him be able, upright and conscientious, of soft speech, gentle and not proud, contented and easily supported, with few cares, whose life is no burden to him ... Let him not do anything unworthy for which others who are wise might criticize him. May all beings be happy and secure! May they be happy at heart!

(Karaniya-metta Sutta)

Probably the two most important influences on the development of contemporary Christian spirituality have been the struggle for justice which has led to the phenomenon of liberation theology in the Third World, and, nearer home, the integration into Christian thinking of many of the insights of psychology and the human sciences. The one is a reminder that all spiritual practice must have a social dimension, the other that a right relationship with God is not to be achieved without first learning to be at home with oneself. However far apart they may seem, they have this in common: social as much as psychological conflict inhibits the interior and communal harmony which it is the aim of spirituality to achieve.

All the forms of spirituality which I have spoken of – ritual, mysticism, devotion – have been intended to illustrate this theme. Thus in the last chapter I tried to show that the real person only grows when the petty ego dies, when the self-centred individual becomes conscious of being integrated into a great network of persons who are themselves united into God. No doubt a psychologist could wax eloquent on this theme, noting that the process of what Jung called individuation involves an acknowledgement of those areas of darkness in our lives which we would prefer to ignore. In the First Noble Truth the Buddha seeks to acknowledge the reality of suffering and the impermanence of things, seeing things 'as they really are'. Coming to terms with the shadow, what is psychologically 'other', demands a commitment to the full reality of human living, not an abstraction from it.

Enough has been said about this by way of an inter-faith commentary in the last chapter. I finished by remarking that the contemplative attitude promoted by Buddhism can be characterized as a sort of 'active waiting' or an 'active passivity' – the receptivity and openness which leaves us on the threshold of Divine Mystery rather than the sort of desire and grasping which tries to force us over it. Such an attitude can appear, none the less, as an escape from reality. Not even the greatest mystic can avoid a certain dependence on others. Does he or she not have some responsibility for them? Moreover, does not the mystic's experience have implications for life in society and for the life of that society? In this chapter I want to look at the 'active' side of contemplative passivity. If spirituality is the practice of faith, then what part does it play in forming practical attitudes to *this* world?

Visions of Truth: Motivation for Action

One of the more insidious aspects of the dualistic thinking with which I began is the assumption that religion is concerned with a distinct 'spiritual' world. Priests and preachers are often told to concern themselves with what they know about, 'purely' theological questions, such as human salvation and ultimate destiny. We even find the word 'theological', along with the much-abused 'academic', being used by politicians to refer to something irrelevant to the nitty-gritty or everyday living. That images of God and visions of ultimate reality can have an extraordinary power to motivate people to *present* action has been conveniently ignored (though the recent explosion of anger in the Muslim community over *The Satanic Verses* has come as a nasty shock in some parts of our apathetic secularized society). Radical clergy are often dismissed as ignorant, meddlesome nuisances. It is easily forgotten that the vocal few represent only a tiny fraction of the vast majority of ordinary Christians whose world has been formed by the values of the gospel – the Good News that what Christ has revealed of the love of God *actually makes a difference, here and now*. Resurrection may be a future reality, but it is not *just* future.

In a depressingly materialist society any acknowledgement of spiritual or religious values is to be warmly welcomed. But we need to be careful. To repeat: religions are not private belief-systems

111

about unverifiable future realities; they originate in the *faith* of communities which form and affect attitudes to *this* world as well as the next. To divorce the spiritual from the political only compounds the problem. The jibe is often made, by traditionalist clergy and conservative politicians alike, that to be too much concerned for the building of the Kingdom is to take on a secularist mentality. There is clearly an important warning in their criticism, even if, all too often, the really significant points are lost in the welter of rhetoric – from both sides. This is not the place to discuss the origins of the liberation theology movement, but only to note that, if there is one 'sign of the times' which needs careful analysis, it is surely the response of the Church to the cry of the poor and dispossessed. What is happening today in South America and Asia merits more careful attention than the tabloid journalist mentality usually allows. Striving to preserve 'religious values' in our contemporary world need not entail a fundamentalist dualism, on the one hand, or a sell-out to the utopian dreams of Marxism, on the other.

The Signs of the Times

How are religious people to be guided in this struggle? For the Christian an engagement with the 'signs of the time', whether in the dialogue with Western atheism, with the struggle for justice in the Third World, or in the inter-religious encounter, continues the great tradition of Christian theologizing which began with Paul and his sermon to the Areopagites described in the Acts of the Apostles. The message of this story is not so much that the gospel has to be adapted so that different people can hear and understand; translation is a more complicated business than finding appropriate alternatives for specific words. Rather, the universal truth which the gospel proclaims has to find a home in different milieux. The fact that Paul's success rate in Athens was minimal does not make the enterprise invalid. Any dialogue, especially the dialogue with contemporary culture, must build on what is already there – but it must also challenge and question that culture. This is the heart of mission. Certain basic principles are at work, the most important of which is the recognition that Christian living and spirituality are about achieving wholeness, about harmonizing all aspects of our lives, not putting them into carefully sanitized

112

compartments. Christians do violence to themselves and to the integrity of the Kingdom of God if they think otherwise.

What role does an inter-faith spirituality play in the articulation of such a very Christian idea as the Kingdom of God? Earlier I spoke about the interaction of prophetic and mystical religion and how the latter can correct some of the excesses of the former. Religious motivations are sometimes based on very different premisses – which is not to say that they are all equally valid or beyond criticism. Take, for example, two very different reactions to the debate about the blasphemy law, occasioned by Muslim anger over the publication of *The Satanic Verses*. Shabbir Akhtar, Community Relations Officer in Bradford, wrote that 'the fact that post-Enlightenment Christians tolerate blasphemy is a matter for shame, not for pride. It is true, of course, that God can defend himself, but a believer must vindicate the reputation of God and his spokesmen against the militant calumnies of evil.'[1] This is a typically Muslim way of thinking: the believer has a duty to see that God is not mocked. Contrast this with what the Buddha says:

> If outsiders speak in dispraise of me, or of the *dharma*, or of the Sangha, you should not on that account either bear malice, or suffer heart-burning, or feel ill-will. If you, on that account, should be angry and hurt, that would stand in the way of your own self-conquest.[2]

This is typically Buddhist: only the controlled, pure state of mind can achieve that true freedom which is *nirvana*. What is typically Christian? Prophetic denunciation of sin? Or are Christians to 'turn the other cheek'? According to their own tradition Christians ought to incline to the latter – if for no other reason than that the prophet who listens, and reacts, with the dispassionate attentiveness of the mystic has more chance of being heard. But much will depend on the circumstances, on what is appropriate at the time, and on how conscious the prophet-mystic is of his or her reasons for acting.

In an earlier chapter I made the point that religion is often trivialized by being turned into the ultimate sanction for morality. If people do not believe in God, it is said, what basis is there for moral action? The fact that there are, and always have been, many people who reject belief in God and yet lead lives of high moral integrity seems not to matter. If we think we need some sort of authoritative code of practice in order to act morally then we have a very limited notion of what it means to be human. One does not need a religious faith in order to know what is right.

Now the basis of morality is not my subject; I willingly leave that to the philosophers. I am more concerned with the relationship between morality and religion. In what follows I do not want to trot out an account of Buddhist or Christian behaviour but a consideration of the relationship between what people do and what people believe. The aim will be to show how practice and theory interact, how a vision of the Truth acts not as a source of moral truths but as a source of motivation.

Rejoicing in Freedom

We can begin by returning to the question noted above, one we have been considering throughout this book: What is the purpose of religion? If it is not to enforce morality then what is religion for? It would be naive to think that religious practice is just a matter of doing good and avoiding evil. The very human problem, which religion seeks to address, is precisely our *incapacity* to do good and avoid evil. In all religions we are presented with admirable ethical precepts and a vision of an ideal society, but no code of conduct is perfect, nor can it cater for all eventualities. Ethical dilemmas abound, in business, in medicine, in everyday living, in which we are faced not with avoiding what is clearly bad but with choosing between what are often perceived to be different goods. How do we tell what, in any particular situation, is right? Moreover, and perhaps most importantly, how do we cope when good is *not* done and evil, willingly or unwillingly, is allowed to take over? How are we to deal with the fact that people do not live up to their ideals?

Religions deal with these questions in very different ways. Not surprisingly the mystical religions of India and the Far East emphasize personal autonomy and commitment. The prophetic religions, on the other hand, rely on the authority of the revealed tradition. Thus the Buddha-sangha, the community of monks, is regulated by the *vinaya*, the discipline which lays down an exact code of practice. These rules of conduct are an elaboration of the five basic precepts which every Buddhist takes along with the three refuges – the Buddha, the *dharma* and the Sangha. The form is worth noting:

Honour to the Buddha, the worthy one, the fully enlightened one.

I go to the Buddha for refuge.

I go to the *dharma* for refuge.

I go to the Sangha for refuge.

For a second time I go to the Buddha, *dharma*, Sangha for refuge.

For a third time ...

I undertake the precept to abstain from taking life.

I undertake the precept to abstain from taking what is not given.

I undertake the precept to abstain from wrong conduct in sexual desires.

I undertake the precept to abstain from telling lies.

I undertake the precept to abstain from intoxicating liquors which occasion heedlessness.

For a Buddhist of the ancient Theravada school this is the equivalent of reciting the Christian Creed, what makes a Buddhist a Buddhist, a sort of statement of intent. As is often pointed out, the individual freely undertakes a certain course of conduct; it is not imposed from without. It contrasts with the special revelation found in the Hebrew Bible where Yahweh speaks directly to his people and bestows on them a special gift, the Torah, which sets them apart from the Gentiles. The ten commandments, for example, are imperatives which are to be accepted, not chosen. In the same way Muslims are subject to an external law. The *Shari'a* dominates the everyday lives of the Umma. It is an essential expression of Muslim identity – a body of laws to which an individual must go in order to determine how he or she should behave in society. How does Christianity compare with these two very different approaches?

Let us take the prophetic religions first. In Christianity the relationship between religion, morality and law is rather different from the other two 'religions of the book'. In the last chapter I noted that the teaching of Jesus – and more particularly that of Paul – contains plenty of moral injunctions. Understood correctly, however, they are not a code of conduct in the same way that the *Shari'a* or the Jewish Torah are. The Sermon on the Mount, for instance, does not seek to rewrite the ten commandments, adding, subtracting, providing new laws for a new situation. Rather Jesus makes an invitation to his disciples to respond generously to his invitation to attempt *now* to live the life of the kingdom of God, that is to say under the reign of the Father. Jesus is portrayed as a new Moses, proclaiming a new revelation which fulfils rather than replaces what has gone before. However, in the long list of precepts in which Jesus contrasts his teaching with Moses, the emphasis is less on what is said than on *who* is saying it. 'You have heard that it was said ... But *I* say to you ...' Jesus is not proclaimed as the new Moses, for that would make him another prophet – admittedly a very superior prophet, but a prophet none the less. The gospels see more in the significance of Jesus than this. The various Christologies which the evangelists develop all try to answer the question raised early on in Mark's version of the Good News: 'Who is this?' The experience of the early Church was that in Jesus God's power was at work in an extraordinary way, to the extent that those who allowed themselves to come under his influence found their lives transformed. 'In Christ', as Paul puts it, the disciples find a new motivation for living, a motivation summed up in the imperative of the new commandment, to 'love one another even as I have loved you' (John 13.34). This is not meant to abolish the old law, which remains God's gift, but to provide the possibility of its fulfilment through the change of heart which the Spirit of Christ brings.

It is not, then, that the 'spirit of the law' is to be opposed to the 'letter' (which usually means the letter being conveniently ignored), but that the Holy Spirit enables those conscientiously seeking to live a life of integrity and generosity to see beyond the letter, to cope with ethical dilemmas and to learn to live with their own failure. Such is the purpose of the revelation of what God has done in the life, death and resurrection of Christ and the promise which is already being enacted in the lives of those who respond to the guidance of the Spirit. This is the life of the Kingdom: a response to ideals which are considered *possible* here and now.

Of course, there are Christians who expect to find in the Bible quite explicit guidelines on all aspects of personal and social morality. Strict evangelical theology teaches that human beings find themselves dominated by sin. A fundamental ignorance of God leads to an inner conflict or division which can only be overcome by the revelation of God himself. It is easy to equate this revelation with the norms of conduct found in the biblical texts. That a minority of Christians should follow this line of thinking is hardly surprising when we read the words Paul writes to the Romans: 'I know that nothing good dwells within me, that is, in my flesh. I can will what is right, but I cannot do it' (Rom. 7.18). Paul, however, is not teaching an inner conflict between a good and an evil principle, still less between a spiritual soul and an evil body. Nor does he portray the world as the scene of a great Manichean battle in which the powers of light are forever locked in conflict with the forces of darkness. Paul's gospel is contained in the hymn of praise to God which climaxes chapter eight of the same epistle: 'I am sure that neither death, nor life, nor angels, nor principalities, nor things present, nor things to come, nor powers, nor height, nor depth, nor anything else in all creation, will be able to separate us from the love of God in Christ Jesus our Lord' (Rom. 8.38-9). This is the joy of a new-found freedom, not the dependency which chains itself to an unquestionable code.

Morality, Prayer and Meditation

My point is that the Bible is not to be regarded as a fund of moral norms for insiders any more than it may serve as a resource from which may be culled apologetic proof texts to be used against outsiders. This is where Christianity differs most obviously from Islam, a difference most marked in attitudes to the relationship of 'Church' and 'State'. Most Christians do not expect – or want – to live in a society which is governed by 'Christian law' in the way that Muslims would hope to live in a society governed by the *Shari'a*. Muslims find a secular pluralist society deeply threatening as it seems to be based on an ideology which is thoroughly antagonistic to everything that Islam stands for: the sovereignty and oneness of God in human affairs. Any community of faith, particularly the Christian, will feel a certain sympathy for the Muslim predicament, but it will be a sympathy qualified by the bitter experience of history which has sometimes seen faith imposed as a sign of ideological or nationalist conformity. Christians would now insist that faith should be a matter of free commitment, but it was not always so.

This does not mean that there can be no such thing as a Christian society or that Christians would not want to live in a society which is governed by Christian ideals. It does not follow, however, that society will be governed by 'Christian law' – for there can be no such thing. The role of Christian faith is not to provide a legislative authority for society but to perform a critical function within society: to question accepted practice and to keep pressing for recognition within society of genuinely Christian ideals. This brings us to the heart of the matter: Jesus teaches a vision of a just society but, more important, through the guidance of the Spirit develops a motivation which enables people to go on striving to realize the values of the gospel.

Buddhism too, despite giving rise to as great a civilization as Islam, does not presume to provide a blueprint for society. Like Christianity it teaches a moral code which is more a vision of perfected human relationships than a set of laws or even guidelines for human living. To read accounts of Buddhist ethics is rather a tedious business. Lists of virtues and precepts are locked in uneasy tension with lengthy description of offenses and penalties. The Sanskrit word *śila*, which is usually translated as morality, has the sense of habit of living or conduct. Together with *prajña* and *samadhi*, wisdom and concentration, it makes up the three trainings, a basic summary of Buddhist practice. In the Noble Eightfold Path, Right Thought, Right Speech, Right Action and Right Livelihood can be put under the general heading of *śila*, which thus refers to a general discipline of duties to be performed and actions to be avoided. There is nothing remarkable about the lists which spell out *śila* except their length and complexity; the precepts mentioned earlier are to be found in some form in all religions. Again, it is the form or the context rather than the content which is to be noted: Buddhism sees morality not as a preparation for enlightenment, a stage in the progress of the Middle Way, but as an integral part of the single process of learning to see things as they really are. Immediately, then, our attention is drawn to the realism we spoke of earlier; the person who practises mindfulness will be the person of integrity who pursues *śila*, and vice versa.

The two go together. This is because Buddhism is very much a 'mind-culture' – by which should not be understood a body-soul dualism, a sort of Indian Cartesianism, but very much the opposite; external action and internal motivation must be brought into harmony. The Buddha inherited the strict cause and effect theory which dominates all forms of Indian ethical thinking. What we do will have an inevitable and predictable result; what we are now is already conditioned by what we have done. This law of *karma* originates in the ritualistic thinking of the Veda and, in a fatalistic sort of way, can be used to explain human failure and inequality. The

Buddha taught, however, that there is something more basic than good or bad action, namely good or bad desire. What we *want* makes an action morally meritorious or demeritorious. 'It is mental volition', he said to his disciples, 'that I call *karma*. Having willed, one acts through body, speech or mind' (*Anguttara Nikaya* 3.145). In the ancient collection of texts called the Dhammapada, it is said that 'He who speaks or acts from a mind defiled, that one suffering follows as a wheel the foot that leads it.' 'Mind', says the same collection, 'precedes all things; all things have mind foremost and are mind-made.' All improvements or retrograde steps have their beginnings in the mind, in the intention of the individual whether that intention proceeds to external manifestation then or at a later date. Hence the importance of being aware of, and of controlling, one's thoughts as well as actions: through the practice of mindfulness morality merges into meditation.

Clearly there is a danger in Buddhism, as with all meditative spiritualities, that attention is focused on subjective rather than objective needs. Personal restraint is seen to be more desirable than positive action if only because it better preserves that tranquillity without which meditation becomes impossible. Even the 'positive' forms of Buddhist meditation, for instance on the four *brahmaviharas*, the qualities of compassion which make up the 'divine abodes', can be self-regarding in the worst sense. A forest-dwelling monk whom I met in Śri Lanka claimed that his favourite form of meditation was 'radiating loving-kindness', but his increasingly irritable answers to my few enquiries showed that his practice, if not his meditative skills, was distinctly limited. Crabbed, stunted personalities are to be found in all religions; the capacity to master meditative techniques is no guarantee of moral excellence. Almost inevitably exercises which focus on internal processes are going to develop in some people a sense of isolation and independence, not an expansion of the personality in which selfishness is overcome. The wonder is that this happens so rarely. My bad-tempered monk was an exception, not the rule. The meditation techniques which we discussed earlier normally lead to a forgetting of the ego, in which self dies and a sense of the relatedness of the whole created order comes alive. The world of the other plays a significant part in meditation, drawing a person out, not isolating him or her within.

It is important to note that this is a single process. In the New Testament Jesus is often portrayed at prayer to the Father. He withdraws apart from the crowds, not in order to escape from pressure, but to draw strength from his loving relationship with the Father. Even, and perhaps especially, in Gethsemane his prayer is focused on the mission to which he is called: 'Father, if thou art willing, remove this cup from me; nevertheless not my will, but thine, be done' (Luke 22.42). This is the mark of dependence on God. More specifically, Jesus teaches through his example that the whole of Christian living is marked by this double movement of withdrawal and return; time spent in the presence of God leads to time spent in the presence of one's fellow human beings – and vice versa. There is thus this double commitment, to God and to the other. This pattern of experience sets up all sorts of tensions which are only resolved with great difficulty. Hence the many spiritualities – formal attempts at resolution – which the tension has caused to develop. The Benedictine tradition, for instance, emphasizes the regularity of prayer and work, the constant repetition of the office and the routine of the day contributing to a certain stability from which others can draw strength. Ignatian spirituality, on the other hand, brings prayer and mission together in a quite different way. The following of the poor Christ, striving to build the Kingdom of justice and peace, is seen in terms of companionship. Withdrawal for prayer takes place in the middle of the action, as it were, in direct imitation of the way Jesus expresses his dependence on the Father.

Wisdom and Compassion

These spiritualities are variations on a theme: the central Christian conviction that only in God is the true motivation for action to be found. Although the language is very different, something similar is to be found in Buddhism. It is worth recalling the story of the Buddha's enlightenment and its immediate aftermath. The thought occurs to him that the *dharma* which he has attained to is 'profound and hard to see'. He reflects on the lack of understanding of ordinary people; they are too slow and ignorant; if he tries to teach them 'they would not understand me, and that would be wearying and troublesome for me'. His immediate decision is to keep silent, for who can possibly understand? Then, according to the tradition, the supreme god Brahma appears before the Buddha and pleads on behalf of suffering humanity that he proclaim the life-giving law which he has discovered. The Buddha is persuaded by the god's entreaties and replies: 'Wide open are the portals of the Deathless. Let those who hear show faith.' Thus begins the Buddha's search for people capable of understanding the subtleties of the law, culminating in the first sermon to the five ascetics in the deer-park at Sarnath, the 'setting in motion of the wheel of truth'. The role that Brahma plays in this celebrated legend should not delay us. It is not intended to make the god more important than the Buddha but, rather, the opposite: only a fully enlightened one, who has seen the truth, can teach others. The story, preserved in the language of Indian mythology, tells how the Buddha is, at once, enlightened about the truth and empowered to proclaim it. Or, to put it another way, seeing the truth is to feel oneself united with all those sentient beings who are part of that truth. In Buddhist terms, the key qualities of wisdom, *prajña*, and compassion, *karuna*, are interdependent.

This teaching would seem to be implicit in the typically Buddhist form of meditation known as the 'setting up of mindfulness'. The meditator cannot be mindful of all the various aspects of experience in the manner taught by the Buddha without also becoming deeply conscious of the needs of others. Compassion grows with insight and wisdom. In the Mahayana tradition we find this expressed in the devotional Lotus Sutra, a composite text which dates from around 200 CE. Tradition has it that the Buddha proclaimed it just before the final *nirvana* as the most appropriate teaching for the final age when religion finds itself in a state of decay. The Buddha is presented in the text as the one who out of compassion adapts the message to the needs and dispositions of different hearers. This is what is known as his 'skill in means', a typically Buddhist concept which shows compassion at work, deliberately accommodating the one *dharma* to varying needs. To an extent such accommodation distorts the truth, but the various forms which the Buddha's teaching takes should be seen as *temporary* means which can soon be discarded in the same way that a raft is left behind when the river has been crossed.

What the Buddha aims to do is explained in various parables – for example, the burning house. The children of a loving father are playing in a house, completely oblivious to the fire which has just broken out and threatens to destroy them. The father's warnings go unheeded. Only when he lures them out with the promise of better toys to play with do they realize how narrowly they have escaped a nasty death. Thus it is with the Buddha's teachings. Doc-

121

trine has a practical function: to lead people to enlightenment. In both the Theravada and the Mahayana traditions, in their different ways, the ideal is represented by the person of the *bodhisattva*, literally the 'being-for-enlightenment', who postpones his own enlightenment in order to help others. A useful image is that of the shepherd, not the good shepherd of the Bible who leads the sheep, but a shepherd who comes last, gathering in the flock from behind, as it were. This is 'skill in means' – the capacity to lead without seeming to lead. It is illustrated vividly in the Lotus Sutra by another parable which recalls Jesus' story about the prodigal son. Here the long-lost son returns by accident to the city where his father is ruler. Everything has changed and he fails to recognize his father. The father, however, knows the son and, despite the great distance between them, out of the depths of his compassion goes to infinite pains to reveal himself without frightening the wretched son to death. Gradually he gives him more and more important tasks and eventually, when he has gained his son's confidence, lets him know his true identity. This is the Buddha-nature.

The Christian, of course, begins not with the restoration of a sort of primal vision of truth but with the revelation of what God has done in Christ. And what is learned through prayer, meditation and devotion is not how to exercise compassion for all sentient beings but how, first of all, to *receive* the love of God which is then shared with others. It is possible, however, to exaggerate the differences. For all its gnostic tendencies Buddhism sets compassion alongside wisdom as the two inseparable aspects of a single ideal: knowing and acting are one. In both traditions vision leads to action – but it is an action which is motivated by compassion. The enlightenment of the Buddhist, the conversion of the Christian, are not private experiences. They flow, as it were, into the world. Perhaps more important, they are formed in the world, in company with the rest of suffering humanity.

Notes

1 The *Guardian*, 27 February 1989.
2 Quoted in a 'Note on Blasphemy by the Office of the Western Buddhist Order', part of *Law, Blasphemy and the Multi-Faith Society*, the Report of a seminar held under the joint auspices of the Commission for Racial Equality and the Interfaith Network (London: Commission for Racial Equality, 1990), pp. 88–9.

CHAPTER 10

Learning to Speak of God

Truth alone conquers, not falsehood. By truth is laid out the path leading to the gods by which the sages whose desire is satisfied ascend to where is the highest repository of truth.

(Mundaka Upanishad 3.1.6)

In Buddhism the qualities exhibited by the *bodhisattva*, wisdom and compassion, are so closely linked that they appear as the two sides of a single ideal. If there is a Christian equivalent, it is to be found in what the liberation theologians emphasize: the faith which does justice. In both Buddhism and Christianity a vision of truth leads to motivation for action. All faiths would subscribe to the great upanishadic claim that 'Truth alone conquers'; without the conviction that their experience speaks of what is true, communities of faith would cease to exist. But how do religious people (not always renowned for breadth of vision and openness of heart) learn to recognize truth and, more particularly, to act truthfully? We have spoken about different ways of practice which I have interpreted as modes of knowing. But what of the Ultimate Mystery to which they all point? The symbols of faith are clearly crucial to the practice of faith. The way people picture the essential relatedness of the Divine and the world is going to have an important effect on the way they treat that world – and each other.

God and the World: Creation and History

To know the Ultimate is to be able to speak of that Mystery in human terms. This is done most obviously through familiarity with the language of a religious tradition. At the same time, it is necessary to recognize the limits of the language which is used. And yet, however different the languages with which people try to speak of God, however diverse the practices to which those languages give rise, both mystical and prophetic traditions are trying to come to terms with the same theological question (there is only one, from which all else arises).

The question is not exclusively Christian. Hindus and Buddhists (using very different language) ask it too. In Christian terms: How does one speak of God and creation in such a way as to safeguard the freedom of both? How is God, the Ultimate, to remain the 'Other', without being constrained and therefore limited by an 'involvement' in the finiteness of creation? And how, in the face of this Divine Mystery, is our human nature to retain a substantive reality which allows for a real fulfilment of the hopes and aspirations which we share – which makes us more than mere puppets in a divine game? To put it more simply: How does one allow God to be God and our human nature to be truly human?

We have seen that mystical and prophetic religion begin the search for an answer from opposite directions, as it were. In India one does not have to struggle to uncover the signs of the divine presence; the whole of creation reveals God, for nothing counts as profane. On a visit to India some years ago, I was woken up very early in the morning by some loud music being blasted out across the countryside. On enquiring later in the day from a friendly local what was going on I was told that the music was from the local temple. 'They are waking up the god,' he said. Such a disconcertingly anthropomorphic attitude to the Hindu gods is too easily dismissed as 'pantheism'; rather it conceals a profound sense of the Divine at the very heart of the world. To 'wake up the god' is to begin each day with a special ritual which celebrates the divinity which exists at the heart of the world.

Prophetic religions, on the other hand, begin with a response to God's self-revelation, a response which, as we have noted, includes liturgical celebration, different forms of contemplative prayer and a loving response to the experience of sharing in God's gifts. Compared with Christianity, Indian spirituality is, in the first place, not so much a response to the creative and redemptive acts of God but a celebration of the immediacy of the Divine, with hymns to nature and the various powers and forces, some benign, some not, which the world appears to contain. *Karma, jñana* and *bhakti-yoga*, need to be understood against this background.

This, perhaps, is the first and most significant way in which Hindu attitudes to the world differ from more familiar Judeo-Christian notions. The creation story in Genesis is told as if it was a historical event. There is no beginning to God; there is a beginning to creation – that moment at which God decides to create 'out of nothing'. Moving the story on a stage, we note that the sin of Adam is even more obviously portrayed as an actual event which occurs in time. Together with other myths like Cain's slaying of his brother and the confusion of languages which results from the building of the tower of Babel, we get the picture of a God whose benevolent purposes for humankind are thwarted by his own greatest gift – freedom. If the fall is part of human history, then salvation must be seen in these terms too: the intervention of God in history, establishing a covenant with a particular people, and himself being the source of that reconciliation. The assurance of this salvation is depicted by the gifts of the Spirit which descend on the embryo Church at Pentecost, thus reversing the chaos and disharmony of Babel. Salvation is the restoration of a correct relationship with God originally established in the act of creation.

How fair a reading of the biblical tradition this is I must leave to one side. Christians very often speak of the 'history of salvation', a phrase which betrays a very strong sense of God's self-revelation occurring in ordinary human events, indeed in the person of Christ through human life itself. Perhaps surprisingly, however, this has not always produced the positive theology of creation one would expect. There is much to be said for the view that Reformed theology in its concern to safeguard the sovereignty of God and salvation through faith in Christ *alone* has left us with a very negative picture of sinful humanity and largely failed to produce a positive theology of creation. That there is more to the biblical picture than this narrow rendition is clear. One need only think of the more ecstatic of the Psalms – 'The heavens are telling the glory of God' (Ps. 19.1); hardly nature-mysticism, but a far cry from the gloom of prophetic despondency. Today there is a certain vogue for 'creation theology', a necessary corrective to a one-sided theology of sinful humanity's involvement in 'this vale of tears'. In this perspective history and creation should be viewed as complementary, not opposed, sources of our knowledge of the Divine.

Personal and Impersonal Language

We have noted that mystical and prophetic traditions alike have between them produced a vast number of personal images of Divine Reality – Kali, Rama and Krishna, for instance, or the jealous

God of Israel and the Father of Jesus – and a rather more select but equally mysterious assortment of impersonal titles, such as the Buddhist *śunyata* or the upanishadic *brahman*. No religion fits neatly into either bracket. Thus in the later Vedic hymns we encounter questions about the origins of the world: 'What was the base, what sort of raw matter was there, and precisely how was it done, when the All-maker, casting his eye on all, created the earth and revealed the sky in its glory?' (*Rig Veda* 10.81.2). There is speculation about the name of the Ultimate: 'They call it Indra, Mitra, Varuna, Agni, and it is the heavenly bird that flies. The wise speak of what is one in many ways' (*Rig Veda* 1.164.46). But there is also a certain agnosticism, as if the sages are wary of being too specific in their naming of the Ultimate. It is not perhaps surprising that two currents of thinking emerge in later forms of Hinduism: the more philosophical religion of the Vedanta and the various theistic or *bhakti* cults.

The semitic religions, however, display something of the same tension. There is the *Shema*, still the central creed of Judaism: 'Hear, O Israel: The Lord our God is one Lord; and you shall love the Lord your God with all your heart, and with all your soul, and with all your might' (Deut. 6.4–5). This is Emmanuel, 'God-with-us', the God of the people, he who walks in the cool of the evening with Adam, who is persuaded by Abraham to spare the people of Sodom, whose alternating anger and mercy are portrayed, sometimes in vividly anthropomorphic terms, on almost every page of the Hebrew Bible. And yet this God is also distant and infinitely mysterious – as the distinctly ambiguous images of wind and fire indicate.

The first verses of Genesis speak of the Spirit of God, moving like a wind over the face of the waters. God's creative power is revealed in a number of different ways: in the wild wind bending the trees, in the whirlwind which confronts Job and in the breath of life without which things die. Fire is both the medium of judgement and the symbol of holiness. Thus the vision of Isaiah: 'The Lord will come in fire, and his chariots like the stormwind, to render his anger in fury, and his rebuke with flames of fire' (Isa. 66.15); and the voice from the bush which burns without being consumed: 'Do not come near ... for the place on which you are standing is holy ground' (Exod. 3.5). And in the Pentecost story the coming of the Spirit is symbolized both in terms of the sound 'like the rush of a mighty wind' (Acts 2.2) and the tongues of fire which rest on each one of the disciples. Not for nothing is the fire described as 'tongues' – for Jesus' disciples are now empowered to go out and speak, in many languages and tongues, 'as the Spirit gave them utterance' (Acts 2.4). Traditional symbols are privileged means of access to the Divine – but they are not the only way.

The Language of Myth

Earlier we spoke of rituals like pilgrimage which bring alive the symbols of a religion by acting them out – expressing them in terms of those great myths, legends and the stories which forge a link with the world of the past and teach the community of faith how to speak. Mercifully the days are long gone when myths were patronized as the unscientific musings of a primitive people. I have already drawn attention to several myths from the Bible which form the basis for much Christian theology. There are two major sources for Hindu myths: that contained in the Vedic literature, the earliest written source for classical Hinduism, and the great collections made up of the epics, the Mahabharata and Ramayana, and the Puranas, a word which literally means 'ancient'. None of them make for easy reading. They draw on ancient legends, about local god-figures and semi-mythical heroes; they seek to answer people's questions about why things are the way they are.

In South India temples often have their own mythology, to explain their origins. The temple of Palni, for example, perched on a mountain and approached by a long stone stairway forever thronged with devotees and wandering *sadhus*, is dedicated to Murugan the ascetic, a son of Śiva. The story goes that Śiva offered a prize of rare fruit to whichever of his two sons travelled round the world the faster. Murugan started off on his favourite peacock while his brother, the elephant-headed Ganesh, did a ritual walk around his father, explaining that since Śiva was the centre of the entire universe he had fulfilled the task required of him. Śiva gave him the prize, but when Murugan arrived back and discovered how he had been duped, he immediately withdrew in what can only be called a fit of sulks to dwell as an ascetic, brooding on the top of the mountain. There he sits withdrawn from the world, a reminder to the people of the area of the call to solitude and contemplation.

Both the Vedas and the Puranas, not to mention such local legends, record much ancient wisdom as well as more incomprehensible and unlikely exploits. All sorts of different images and stories compete for our attention, some of them quite contradictory. The Western mind often has to resort to the editorial pencil in order to make any sense of them. For the Hindu, however, strict logic comes second. The myths do not aim to be consistent. They are, rather, representative of the assimilative tendency which is fundamental to Indian religion. Everything must find a place in the total scheme of things; to omit anything is to risk losing some element of that complete wisdom and liberation to which everyone aspires. Gods that brood in darkness are as much a part of the reality of the world as gods of light.

Myths of all kinds clearly exercise a great hold over the imagination, feeding the collective memory and providing important insights into the way people conceive of the nature of the Divine. There is, however, a weakness in a highly personalized faith (as the myth of Krishna and the cow-maidens teaches), namely a tendency to place the individual at the centre where, properly, only God belongs. Is there not a danger that the sort of anthropomorphism with which I began – 'waking up the god' – may evacuate the mystery of the 'Totally Other', replacing the Divine with a projection of our self-centred imaginations?

A Shift in Understanding

In the first chapter I argued that all spirituality is about the right ordering – and therefore right correcting – of desire. In this book I have spoken of three forms of spirituality, but together they represent a single process, leading the individual to develop the language of faith which is learned in and through the community into something more personal. Devotional spirituality, in particular, focuses attention on the heart, bringing about a simplification of consciousness which shifts attention back from the individual to the community. This process represents a growth in *self*-understanding, and of the way in which God, the community and the individual are related. But, if there is a growth in the way people worship and pray, then there must also be a change in the way the Divine is conceived. How the various symbols of faith at the heart of different religious traditions are related together is, of course, an extremely complicated business which is not to be dismissed in a few sentences. My concern, however, is less with doctrine than with the practice which expresses faith. Each form of practice has

a part to play in coming to understand the mystery of our existence
– the way of ritual as much as that of meditation or personal devotion.

Religions, mystical and prophetic, contain both personal and impersonal images which are proper to these different spiritualities. And theologians from different faiths recognize two distinct tendencies or approaches to the language of faith. In the *bhakti* tradition of Hinduism Brahman is spoken of as *saguna*, with characteristics, and *nirguna*, without characteristics. Christian theologians have long distinguished the *via negativa* from the *via affirmativa*, the former recognizing that we can never say, positively, what God *is*, only what God is not, the latter based on the imagery and symbolism which can be used *analogically* of God. Both begin, of course, from practice, but the fact that in so many religious traditions the two exist side by side should not obscure the fact that the one provides an important corrective or balance to the use of the other.

The example of Buddhism may give us some clue as to how this shift or 'growth' mentioned earlier may come about. In looking at Buddhism we have already noted that mythological elements surround the basic Buddha-story, trying to give some account of the identity of a Buddha, an 'enlightened' one, *vis-à-vis* the world of human beings and the world of the gods. Thus it is the god Brahma who persuades the Buddha to break his silence. In Buddhism the gods of the Veda are given a limited significance. They are as much subject to the reality of suffering, impermanence and insubstantiality as all those 'sentient beings' whom the Buddha, in his compassion, vows to help with the 'cure' of the Middle Way. There are various myths which are barely disguised bits of Buddhist propaganda, putting the 'old' gods properly in their place. There is, for instance the famous story of the man who wants to know where the four elements, earth, fire, water and wind, go when they fade away. In his meditation he raises himself to the levels occupied by different gods but gets no answer to his questions. Eventually he comes into the presence of Brahma. Again no answer, but his persistence is rewarded when Brahma takes him to one side and whispers to him in private that the other gods expect the great Brahma to know everything, but, 'the truth is, I do not know where those four elements cease leaving nothing behind'. The story is complete when Brahma points to the Buddha who alone can answer the man's question (*Digha Nikaya* 1.221). The gods have their place; they can grant this-worldly favours but they cannot overcome decay, suffering and death.

These myths represent a radical shift in understanding of the nature of the Absolute. It is essential to see where this begins; theory has its origins in practice. Buddhism takes its stand less on a particular concept – still less *image* – of Ultimate Reality than on trying to understand the *way* in which we try to conceive of Ultimate Reality in the first place. Buddhism draws attention to the dangers of projection, the way in which we project a symbol of ourselves on to God or make God in our own image. The Buddha's silence is not a fatalistic agnosticism but a recognition that words are only words, human signs, which can no more contain the Ultimate Mystery than the meditator can touch the majesty of God. To understand this we need to return briefly to the Buddha's teaching, the *dharma*, and examine the role which it plays in Buddhist tradition.

Recognizing the Limits of Language

Earlier I noted that Indian religion is marked by the interaction of two major trends: seeing the Absolute in terms of some sort of mystical state of being or as a personal God. The latter is typical of *bhakti* or devotional religion but currents are already to be discerned in the Vedas and become prominent in the Bhagavad Gita and in the mythology typical of the *Puranas*. The former stems from the period of the Upanishads, very much under the influence of the 'renouncer movement' in reaction to the ritualism of the brahmanical religion. Buddhism follows a similar ideology to that of the wandering *sannyasis* of the upanishadic period: the analysis of the human condition as governed by the inexorable law of *karma*, the practice of *yoga*, and the pursuit of ultimate *moksha* or liberation. In that case was the Buddha 'just another *yogi*' – albeit a rather more successful one? What makes the Buddha unique is not just the enormous compassion he felt and practised towards all 'sentient beings' but his own very definite conception of *dharma*, the truth which is the source of freedom. The Buddha is the compassionate one who teaches people in a way appropriate to their condition, but this should not obscure the fact that he was fully enlightened – which, in Buddhist terms, means that he was guided by a vision of *dharma* which goes beyond adherence to any particular ideology.

What is this *dharma* that the Buddha teaches? Buddhism emerged in, and can only be understood in terms of, the Indian religion of the sixth century BCE – essentially the religion of the Vedas. Buddha was critical of the Vedic tradition but he was no iconoclast; he never doubted the existence of the gods or the spirit world. In fact, as we have seen in the story of his enlightenment, the gods have a role to play; in the various forms of contemporary Buddhism, Theravada and Mahayana, there are plenty of god-figures who are by no means irrelevant to the way people conceive of the Divine. In fact it sometimes comes as a surprise to learn that the religion practised by Buddhists in countries as different as Śri Lanka and Nepal contains elements of ritual, spirit-cults and magic. In Kandy, for example, pilgrimage to the Temple of the Tooth and devotion to the god Kataragama go hand in hand. What are strictly 'Buddhist' and 'Hindu' are not rivals but partners. How are we to understand this juxtaposition of the two? In Buddhism the Buddha's enlightenment is the key experience; thus the gnostic tendency 'controls' the devotional.

Western interpreters – and particularly Christian theologians – have found the concept of *nirvana* something of a puzzle. Is not Buddhism an atheistic creed, or – if that is too strong – hopelessly agnostic about the existence, let alone the nature, of Ultimate Reality? Certainly one view of Buddhism sees it as rejecting any sort of devotional religion and substituting instead a religion of reason. What is recommended is a cool stoicism which aims to overcome humankind's obsession with an unattainable Ultimate. Such interpretations are caricatures which tell us more about the interpreters than they do about Buddhism. The apparent atheism encountered by the first missionaries shocked and disgusted them, but came as a welcome discovery to many post-Enlightenment free-thinkers who thought they had found in Buddhism the rationalist this-worldly humanism of the New Age. *Nirvana* meant extinction. What else could be understood by the central metaphor of the blowing out of the candle-flame? Not all agreed, however. Was it reasonable to believe that millions of people could seriously follow a religion which made annihilation its central tenet? If, it was argued, the desire for salvation is at the heart of all religion, then *nirvana* must approximate somehow to a Christian vision of immortality.

This is not the place to comment on the way in which Christian theological concerns have dominated the debate, projecting some very non-Buddhist ideas into a way of life and thought which needs to be understood on its own terms, not rewritten in order to answer questions it never asked. It is all too easy to assume that *nirvana* must be understood either negatively as the 'blowing out' of the candle-flame which is the human person (an interpretation which is never made in the texts), or positively as a 'state' of salvation, by which is implied some sort of communion with the One, the Divine or God. The former leaves us with a moralistic understanding of religion; the latter tends to the theistic. Neither is correct. *Nirvana* represents an oriental answer to a very oriental question – which is not to say that it does not encourage us to focus on a question which is also asked by the prophetic religions.

The Buddha's enlightenment represents a complete shift in the way that the Absolute is to be conceived – but a shift which, nevertheless, still recognizes that there is a place for the language of personal theism if one is not to lapse into total silence. Gnostic language does not destroy devotional.

The Middle Way to Liberation

The two always go together: the practices of a community of faith which provide the key to understanding its central beliefs, particularly its conception of Ultimate Reality. The truth experienced by the Buddha is not a formula of words but a way of life, or, to be more accurate, the Right View gained from that way of life: the beginning, and in this sense the end, of the Noble Eightfold Path. This is the key to the Middle Way. And it also underlines the significance for the Buddhist of the Sangha, the community of disciples which, with Buddha and *dharma*, make up the three jewels. To be a Buddhist is to declare one's intention to go to Buddha, *dharma* and Sangha for refuge or protection. This third is not some sort of commitment to the formal structure of a Buddhist Church. The Sangha is more than that; it is the vehicle without which *dharma* ceases to exist. The contribution of the monks to society is to teach, to be the living embodiment of Buddhist ideals and the sign of the compassionate Buddha's continuing presence in the world. However much that teaching may have been elaborated, under various pressures and influences, the Sangha embodies the sense of loyalty to the tradition which is at the heart of all religious traditions. In the case of Buddhism this loyalty is to a certain teaching about the way to liberation – the Middle Way – and the Right View from which it is inseparable.

To say that this teaching is practical is only half the story. It is true that, when he was asked about Ultimate Questions, such as the nature of *nirvana* or the existence of the individual after death, the Buddha 'replied' with the famous silence – a refusal to be drawn which speaks more eloquently of the Absolute than many a learned treatise. This is not to say that his teaching of *dharma* does not have a positive role to play. For the Buddhist linguistic forms are strictly functional. Like a raft, they are to be used to enable the traveller to cross to the further shore; once on the other side they can safely be abandoned. Buddha's pragmatism, as we have already noted, should not be interpreted as meaning that Right View is irrelevant to the genuine pursuit of enlightenment. Right View is not a philosophical 'theory' about the way things are but an acceptance of *what is*, the way things are, not the way we *think* they are.

Mindfulness is the heart of Buddhist meditation – a quality of awareness of the present which is needed to enhance the Right View. To begin on the Way the teaching of the Buddha must be taken on trust, though faith is never enough; it must lead to knowledge. This vision is guided by the insight attributed to the night of the Buddha's enlightenment: the realization that everything we experience is caused or conditioned by something else. Everything we touch, see, taste, smell, everything of which we can speak, is dependent on previous causes. What Buddhists call by the cumbersome title of the 'Law of Conditioned Origination' is simply the working out of the First Noble Truth: everything is *dukkha*, 'suffering', impermanent and insubstantial. This is the truth which the Buddhist learns to develop through the living out of the Noble Eightfold Path into the *prajñaparamita*, literally the 'wisdom that goes beyond', or the perfection of wisdom.

Such a wisdom is not an esoteric 'gnosis' – a sort of private insight into the 'nature of things' granted to the élite meditator. Buddha always claimed that he spoke openly and kept nothing back. Least of all did he teach any sort of ideology or 'system'; in fact attachment to dogmatic views is roundly condemned. What Buddha seems to have rejected, however, is not this view or that but the very dogmatism which adherence to one view imposes unreflectingly on all people. It is easy to see why. It is desire and grasping of all kinds – including prejudices masquerading as philosophical opinion – that pin us to the wheel of rebirth and which inhibit the final and perfect release which is *nirvana*.

We cannot study God. The Ultimate is not a matter of empirical observation. For the Buddha, all that we experience is conditioned; indeed nothing exists which is not in flux. Is it possible to speak of an unconditioned? Most certainly, but in Buddhist terms all we can say about the unconditioned is that *it is*. In a sense, to speak of *nirvana* is to defeat the object of the Middle Way – which, quite simply, is to know the truth. If there is no way of speaking about the unconditioned then we are either forced into silence or, failing that, into a careful criticism of the tendency to project a sometimes very human image on to God or to reduce the unconditioned into a speculative formula.

Spiritual Practice: A Middle Way

This little excursus is intended as a final illustration of my theme: that knowledge comes not just through study of the ancient traditions but through various forms of religious practice. Buddhism is a gnostic tradition – to the extent that its origins are to be found within the Indian tradition of *jñana-yoga*. This is not to say, however, that the other two forms of spirituality are not to be found; 'gnosis', as I have argued, is not to be understood in a narrow or exclusive way. Similarly Christianity is a devotional tradition but includes both ritual and meditative prayer. Christ is the centre of Christian faith but Christ describes himself as 'the way, and the truth, and the life' (John 14.6). However different in form and practice, life in Christ is as much of a journey of faith as the Buddha's Middle Way. Devotion leads – but it will always be a devotion which desires to be led 'into all the truth' (John 16.13).

What, however, is represented in both Buddhism and Christianity – and in other faiths as well – is a constant interaction, a shift or movement from one to another as individuals and communities try to come to terms with their experience and the questions which that experience raises. Each religious tradition has developed a number of ways of expressing and practising faith, ways of understanding the truth which 'alone makes free'. None of the three different yet complementary ways has a monopoly of religious wisdom. Both prophet and mystic have something to say about the search for truth.

All spirituality is about the right ordering of desire – that quality without which no one can begin but which all too easily can lead the unwary into falsehood, not truth. As the author of the Mundaka Upanishad puts it, only the sages 'whose desire is satisfied' can be said to know the truth. This happens when asceticism, the methodical structure of practice, is brought into harmony with the vision of the ideal or goal. Taken together, the ways of liturgy, meditation and devotion balance, challenge and question the various conflicting and disordered desires of the seeker after truth. Taken individually, they run the risk of distortion: prophetic religion taking its stand on obedience to the revealed Word, mystical taking refuge in a plethora of images of the imageless One. People of faith go astray when they dogmatically insist on avoiding any dialogue between the two.

Such a dialogue is essential if faith is to be mature and the desire for truth is not to be substituted by something less than truthful, such as the craving for power or the thirst for 'experience'. Whether we conceive of the divine-human relationship in terms of obedience, mystical intuition or love, there can be no limit to the ways of knowing. And if God is 'always greater' then there can be no limit to what is to be known about God.

Glossary

Atman: 'Essence or principle of life'; in the Upanishads used to denote the eternal, non-material centre of personality.

Bhagavan: 'Lord'; in Hindu theistic systems the generic title for the personal Absolute; e.g. Krishna, as in the Bhagavad Gita and Bhagavata Purana.

Bhakti: 'Devotion'; has the sense of being attached to or sharing, hence 'loyalty'; in Hinduism, when directed towards the Lord, *Bhagavan,* includes various forms of devotion and religious love.

Bodhisattva: 'Enlightenment being'; i.e. a being who is destined to become a Buddha; in Mahayana schools particularly represents the ideal quality of the Buddha as the compassionate teacher.

Brahman: 'Cosmic or all-pervading power'; in Hinduism generally refers to the Absolute, or transcendental state of being; in some of the Upanishads conceived of as identical with *Atman.*

Brahmin: Not to be confused with *Brahman* above; the *brahmin* is the first in the hierarchy of classes; in Hinduism the representative not just of the ritual dimension but also of learning and the orthodox interpretation of the Vedic tradition.

Dharma: 'Truth, law, justice, teaching'; exact meaning depends on context; comes from verbal root with sense of to uphold or bear; hence literally means bearer, whatever upholds or supports.

Dukkha: 'Suffering'; literally that which is difficult to bear; in Buddhism the first of the Four Noble Truths; refers not just to pain but to the unsatisfactory nature of existence in general.

Gurdwara: Literally 'home of the *guru*': the Sikh temple which houses the Guru Granth Sahib, the collection of Sikh scriptures.

Jñana: 'Knowledge'; highest knowledge, insight or wisdom which leads to *moksha.*

Karma: 'Action'; from a verbal root meaning to act or do; in early forms of Hinduism originally refers to the action of the sacrificial ritual but then extended to cover all intentional acts which have moral consequences.

Karuna: 'Compassion'; the most important motivation behind the action of the *bodhisattva.*

Mahayana: Literally 'great vehicle'; school of Buddhism which arose several centuries after the death of the Buddha; more liberal socially and speculative philosophically than the earlier conservative schools which Mahayanists referred to, pejoratively, as *Hinayana,* 'lesser vehicle'.

Moksha: 'Liberation'; in Indian religions the generic term connoting freedom, a transcendental state opposite to *samsara,* which different traditions may specify further; e.g. Hindu theistic schools may speak of *moksha* as union with the Lord, *Bhagavan.*

Nirvana: Literally 'extinction'; the most important Buddhist term for *moksha,* the height of Buddhist aspirations: the basic metaphor at work refers to the blowing out of a fire and thus to the extinction of those factors which hinder *nirvana.*

Purana: 'Ancient stories'; in Hinduism vast groups of texts on the whole concerned with Bhagavan, developing mythologies and genealogies used within *bhakti* traditions.

Qur'an: The Muslim scriptures preached by the prophet Muhammad (d. 632 CE), perceived by him and by Muslims today as the literal, unchangeable words of God, uncreated and eternal, superseding all earlier scriptures.

Samsara: 'Round of rebirth'; key concept in both Hinduism and Buddhism; from verbal root meaning to flow and therefore referring to the continuous process of life, death and rebirth or the world of contingent reality.

Sangha: Literally 'congregation'; the community of the Buddha's monks, the third of the three jewels and three refuges (with Buddha and *dharma*).

Shari'a: 'Path', the Islamic code of law, based chiefly on the Qur'an and the Sunna (the practice of Muhammad); regulating the religious, political, social, domestic, and private life of Muslims.

Śruti: Literally 'hearing'; revealed knowledge contained in the Vedic corpus of scripture, the collections of hymns, the sacrificial commentaries and the Upanishads.

Śunyata: 'Emptiness'; in the philosophical schools of the Mahayana a term developed from the earlier doctrine of *anatmavada* (lack of self) to show that all things are relative, that all objects lack inherent existence.

Theravada: 'Teaching of the Elders'; name of the only surviving one of the early Buddhist schools called collectively the *Hinayana* by the Mahayanists. Claims to have preserved the earliest teachings of the Buddha.

Umma: 'Islamic community', seen as a religious and political unity, transcending national loyalties, owing allegiance to God and to the prophet Muhammad, in continuity with the seventh-century *Umma* of Mecca and Medina.

Upanishad: The *Vedanta* or 'end of the Veda', the final part of the philosophical treatises which sum up and conclude the Hindu *śruti*, or revelation.

Yoga: Literally 'yoking together' in order to gain control; comes to refer to a system of meditative exercises which are intended to cultivate the faculties of the mind so that the practitioner, or *yogi*, can gain an intuitive mystical experience or *jñana*.